THE
LITTLE RED
WRITING
BOOK

20 POWERFUL PRINCIPLES
OF STRUCTURE, STYLE,
& READABILITY

BRANDON ROYAL

W

DIGEST BOOKS
nnati, Ohio
ritersdigest.com

Visit our Web site at www.writersdigest.com for information on more
resources for writers.

To receive a free weekly e-mail newsletter delivering tips and updates
about writing and about Writer's Digest products, register directly at our
Web site at http://newsletters.fwpublications.com.

11 10 09 08 07   5 4 3 2

Library of Congress has catalogued hardcover edition as follows:

Royal, Brandon
  The little red writing book: 20 powerful principles of structure, style,
  and readability / by Brandon Royal.
      p. cm.
1-58297-336-9
    1. English language—Rhetoric. 2. English language—Style. 3. Report
    writing. I. Title.

PE1408.R775 2004   2004047772
808'.042—dc22   CIP

ISBN-13: 978-1-58297-521-4 (pbk.: alk. paper)
ISBN-10: 1-58297-521-3 (pbk.: alk. paper)

Edited by Jane Friedman
Designed by Lisa Buchanan
Production coordinated by Robin Richie

ACKNOWLEDGMENTS

Many individuals — teachers, peers, family, friends, foes, and fellow authors — have influenced my writing development. I am grateful and mention the following with cheer: Erika Archer, Harry Davis, Scott Dunklee, Tony Grey, Kerstin Hall, John Holmes, Douglas McGill, Mitch Presnick, Maxine Rodburg, Richard Stern, Paul Strahan, Julia Travers, Lee Yih, Cammy Yiu, and Stace, Cory, Walter, and Mary Royal.

The journey from submitted manuscript to available product is wondrous. The publisher not only polishes the prose and gives a book its distinctive look but also provides the resources necessary to propel the final package down highways and across oceans. Here I would like to thank Jane Friedman, the executive editor of Writer's Digest Books, for taking on the project and nurturing it to completion. Thanks also to Lisa Buchanan and Julia Groh.

DEDICATION

I think there is truth to the idea that you never really know a subject until you teach it. This book is dedicated foremost to all of my former writing students. The reciprocal nature of teaching ensures that the teacher must always remain a student, and that the student, through his or her questions and struggles, ultimately drives the learning process.

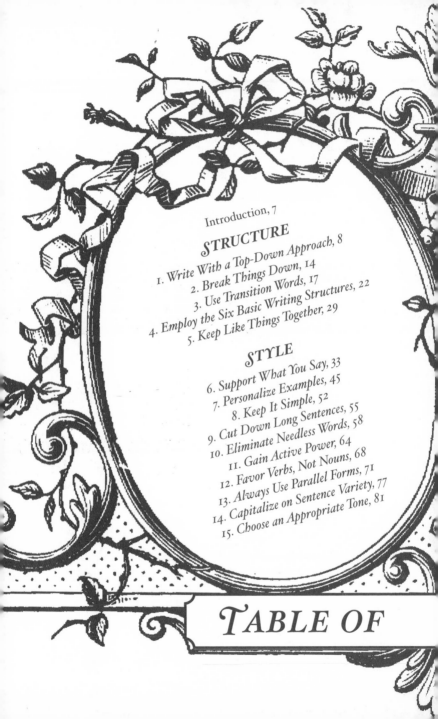

TABLE OF

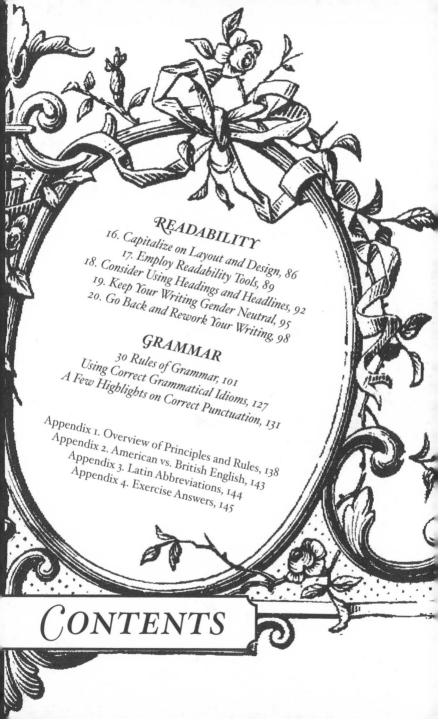

CONTENTS

Introduction

THIS BOOK IS BASED ON A SIMPLE BUT POWERFUL observation: Students and young professionals who develop outstanding writing skills do so primarily by mastering a limited number of the most important related writing principles, which they use over and over again. This statement begs the question: What are these recurring principles? The answer to this question is the basis of this material. Within these pages are twenty immutable principles of writing and thirty commonly encountered rules of grammar and diction.

Writing has four pillars—structure, style, readability, and grammar—and each pillar is like the single leg of a sturdy chair. Structure is about organization and deciding in which order to present your ideas. Style describes how one writes, including how to use specific examples to support what is written. Readability is about presentation, or how to make a document visually pleasing and easy to read. Grammar, including diction, is about expressing language in a correct and acceptable form.

Because of the pervasive nature of writing, this book is suitable for a wide-ranging audience, including writing aficionados from all walks of life. High school and college students can use this material for supplementary study; businesspersons can use this material as a refresher course. Individuals preparing for job placement tests and students preparing for college or graduate entrance exams will benefit from a time-tested review of basic writing principles and rules.

Let's get started.

WRITE WITH A
Top-Down Approach

{Write your conclusion and place it first.}

 Writing done for everyday purposes often falls into the category of expository writing, which includes newspaper articles, college essays, and business memos and letters. Expository writing explains and often summarizes a topic or issue. Strategically, the summary or conclusion should come at the beginning of an expository piece, not at the end. The reader is first told what the writing is about, then given the supporting facts or details. This way, the reader is not left guessing at the writer's main idea.

Whereas the primary purpose of expository writing is to explain or inform, the primary purpose of fiction or creative writing is to persuade or entertain. As far as fiction and creative writing are concerned, it is fine (even desirable) to delay the conclusion, as in the case of a surprise ending. But the hard and fast rule in expository writing is that we should not keep our conclusion from the reader. We should come out with it right away. When our purpose is to explain or inform, don't play, "I've got a secret."

Experienced writing instructors know that one of the easiest ways to fix students' writing is to have them place their conclusions near the top of the page, not the bottom. Instructors are fond of a trick that involves asking students to write a short piece on a random topic and, upon completion, walking up to each student without reading their work, circling the last sentence, and moving it to the very top of the page. In a majority of cases, instructors know that the last lines written contain the conclusion. The technique for correcting this is known as BLOT, or "bottom line on top." It is human nature, and it seems logical, that we should conclude at the end rather than the beginning. But writing should be top-down, structured in the inverted pyramid style. The broad base of the inverted pyramid is analogous to the broad conclusion set forth at the beginning of a piece.

The newspaper industry depends upon the top-down technique of writing. Reporters know that if their stories cannot fit into the allocated space, their editors will cut from the bottom up. Therefore, conclusions generally cannot appear in the last lines, which are reserved for minor details.

Errors of writing often mimic errors in conversation. When we write, we should think about giving the reader a destination first before giving him or her the directions on how to get there. If we fail to do this, we will not get our message across in the most effective way. The value of a top-down approach in real life conversation occurs in the following dialogue.

POOR VERSION

Dialogue between two co-workers:

> *"Sheila, can you do something for me when you're down-town? If you're taking the subway to Main Street, get off and take the first exit out of the subway and walk down to Cross Street. At the intersection of Cross Street and Vine, you'll find Sandy's Stationery store. <u>Can you go in and pick up a couple of reams of A5 paper?</u>"*

BETTER VERSION

Dialogue between two co-workers:

> *Sheila, can you do something for me when you're down-town? <u>I need a couple of reams of A5 paper.</u> The best place to get them is Sandy's Stationery store. You can take the sub-way to Main Street, get off and take the first exit out of the subway and walk down to Cross Street. The store is at the intersection of Cross Street and Vine.*

The conclusion is underlined in each version. Note how annoying the first version can be from the listener's per-spective. If you have encountered a similar situation in real life, you may have felt like screaming. Once you finally find out what the speaker's point is, you might have to ask him or her to repeat everything so you can remember the details. The same holds true for writing. It is just as frustrating when you are reading a piece of writing, and you do not know where the discussion is going.

Conceptually, we want to think in terms of a descending writing structure—one in which we move downhill from conclusion to details rather than uphill from details to conclusion.

Compare the following two versions of the same piece of business writing. In evaluating the two samples, we find that the second one is more top-down in its approach. The conclusion is at the top: "Asia presents the biggest future international market for basic consumer goods if population is used as a measure." Also, the second version uses statistics solely as detail.

LESS EFFECTIVE

Three-fifths of the world's people currently live in Asia, and by the year 2010, some three-fourths of the world's people will live in Asia—from the Middle East to Japan, from Siberia to Indonesia. This population statistic is quite revealing. If, in the year 2010, we selectively and representatively chose four persons from the entire world's people, here is what statistically would happen. One person would be from India, one would be from China, and one more would be from somewhere else in Asia. The fourth person would have to be chosen from all of North America, South America, Europe, Australia, and Africa!

Basic consumer goods represent durable and nondurable daily necessities, including food and cooking utensils, clothing and textiles, toiletries, electronics, home furnishings, and mechanized and miscellaneous household products. <u>Hence, Asia presents the biggest future international market for basic consumer goods if population is used as a measure.</u>

MORE EFFECTIVE

*Asia presents the biggest future international market for
basic consumer goods if population is used as a measure.
Basic consumer goods represent durable and nondurable
daily necessities, including food and cooking utensils, clothing and textiles, toiletries, electronics, home furnishings, and
mechanized and miscellaneous household products.*

*Three-fifths of the world's people currently live in Asia,
and by the year 2010, some three-fourths of the world's people
will live in Asia—from the Middle East to Japan, from
Siberia to Indonesia. This population statistic is quite revealing. If, in the year 2010, we selectively and representatively
chose four persons from the entire world's people, here is what
statistically would happen. One person would be from India,
one would be from China, and one more would be from somewhere else in Asia. The fourth person would have to be chosen
from all of North America, South America, Europe,
Australia, and Africa!*

Now review this piece:

*Hundreds of people packed into the auditorium seats on the
evening of December 29. Being one of twelve opening per-
formers, I was granted the opportunity to dance on stage for
the first time in my life. Although my part only lasted five
minutes, those five minutes became a significant moment in
my life. Ever since rehearsals began two months before, I had
spent many hours practicing on my own, in addition to the
normal rehearsal sessions. Whether on a bus, waiting in a doc-
tor's office, or walking to work, I always had my CD player
on, listening to the music and trying to go through the steps in
my mind over and over again. I was determined to do my
best. Despite my best preparation, my nervousness caused me
to slip during the performance. All of a sudden, my mind*

turned blank. I stood there, not knowing how to react to the music. Fifteen seconds seemed like fifteen hours in a normal day.

The conclusion as underlined above is either well placed or ill placed depending on the writer's purpose in writing the passage. If the purpose is to inform the reader, then it is ill placed because the conclusion should be placed nearer the top. But as this is likely a creative writing piece, meant to entertain, the conclusion can be delayed. Just remember the rule of expository writing that governs everyday writing: Your conclusion should be at or very near the beginning of your written piece.

An airline pilot never leaves the runway without having a destination and flight pattern.

BREAK
Things Down

{Break your subject into two to four parts, and use a lead sentence.}

ASSUMING THAT YOU KNOW WHAT YOU WANT TO write about, you must decide what basic building blocks will comprise your work. You can break your subject into two to four major parts. Three parts are typically recommended, but no more than four categories should be introduced for the sake of simplicity. The classic high school, five-paragraph approach can be used in the setup of any essay or report. The introduction is one paragraph, the body is three paragraphs, and the conclusion is one paragraph. In the example on page 16, all you have to do is supply the colors!

LEAD SENTENCES VS. TOPIC SENTENCES

Once you have broken down your topic into two to four major categories, next you will want to summarize these ideas. Consider using a *lead sentence*, which is similar to a *topic sentence*. Whereas a topic sentence summarizes the contents of a single paragraph within an essay or report, a lead sentence summarizes the contents of an *entire* essay or report. A lead sentence is a topic sentence of topic sentences. Placed at the beginning of a piece, it foreshadows what is to come, highlighting what items will be discussed and, typically, the order in which they will be discussed. Each item in the lead should be developed into at least one separate paragraph within the body of the essay or report. For example, in a personal essay, this sentence could serve as an introduction or lead:

> *I would like to show who I am through a discussion of three special turning points in my personal and career development: when I switched from an English major to an education major, when I spent a year teaching in South Korea, and when I completed my graduate degree in business.*

In a business report, the following could serve as a lead sentence, placed at the beginning of a report:

> *Based on information taken from a recent survey, this report summarizes the three biggest problems that our company faces, namely employee turnover, store thefts, and poor customer service.*

FINDING TWO TO FOUR MAJOR IDEAS

Introduction

Colors make the world bright and full. My favorite colors are green, blue, and yellow. Each one of these colors is special to me._____
_____
_____
_____.

Body

Green is like the green grass that covers the earth._____
_____
_____.

Blue is like the sky._____
_____
_____.

Yellow is like the sun._____
_____
_____.

Conclusion

Green is the most interesting of all of these colors. Even the colors blue and yellow combine to form green._____
_____
_____
_____.

The number three is a magic number in writing—
it is not too small and not too big.

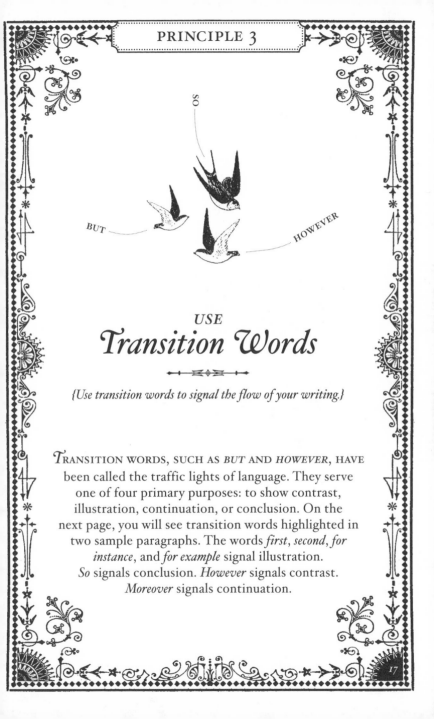

USE
Transition Words

{Use transition words to signal the flow of your writing.}

Transition words, such as *but* and *however*, have been called the traffic lights of language. They serve one of four primary purposes: to show contrast, illustration, continuation, or conclusion. On the next page, you will see transition words highlighted in two sample paragraphs. The words *first*, *second*, *for instance*, and *for example* signal illustration. *So* signals conclusion. *However* signals contrast. *Moreover* signals continuation.

Transition words appear underlined in the following examples.

EXAMPLE 1

> *Time management involves thinking in terms of effectiveness <u>first</u> and efficiency <u>second</u>. <u>Whereas</u> efficiency is concerned with doing a task in the fastest possible manner, effectiveness is concerned with spending time doing the "right" things. Effectiveness is <u>therefore</u> a broader, more useful concept, which questions whether we should even do a particular task.*

EXAMPLE 2

> *The process of evolution takes two distinct forms: organic and exosomatic. In the <u>first</u>, which is commonly called Darwinian evolution, a plant or animal develops a genetic mutation that may be either helpful or harmful. If the change is helpful, the organism is favored by the process of natural selection and flourishes; if it is harmful, the organism suffers and eventually dies out.*
>
> *The whole of what we call human culture, <u>on the other hand</u>, is a result of exosomatic evolution. Such a change may be gradual, <u>but</u> it represents conscious choices that enable human beings to adapt to environments that would otherwise be inimical to their survival.*

THE FOUR TYPES OF TRANSITION WORDS

CONTRAST: "Stop and get ready to turn" • *however* • *but* • *yet* • *on the other hand* • *whereas*

ILLUSTRATION (or enumeration): "Keep going" • *first, second, third* • *for example* • *for instance* • *in fact*

CONTINUATION: "Slow down but keep going" • *furthermore* • *moreover* • *on the one hand* • *undoubtedly* • *coincidentally*

CONCLUSION: "You're about to arrive" • *finally* • *in conclusion* • *so* • *therefore* • *thus* • *as a result*

Exercises

Read the sentences below, arranging them in a manner that makes the most sense in terms of logic and flow. You'll find the suggested solution on page 145.

TOPIC: THE WHALE

1. When people think of ants, on the other hand, they tend to think of hardworking underfed creatures, transporting objects twice their body size to and from hidden hideaways.

2. When most people think of whales, they think of sluggish, obese animals, frolicking freely in the ocean and eating tons of food to sustain themselves.

3. In fact, when we compare the proportionate food consumption of all living creatures, we find that the whale is one the most food-efficient creatures on earth.

4. However, if we analyze food consumption based on body size, we find that ants eat their full body weight everyday, while a whale eats the equivalent of only 1/1,000th of its body weight each day.

5. The whale is the largest mammal in the animal kingdom.

THE SIMPLEST WRITING APPROACH

Here is a sure-fire way to write just about anything. It might not be the most exciting writing structure, but it is clear and it works.

Instructions
1. Take a stance.
2. Write your conclusion.
3. State "There are several reasons for this."
4. Use transition words. Voila.

EXAMPLE TOPIC: RENAISSANCE

The Renaissance Period was the most glorious time in human history. There are several reasons for this.

First,_____

_____Second,_____

_____

_____Third,_____

_____For instance,_____

_____

_____Moreover,_____

_____

_____Finally,_____

_____.

CHRONOLOGICAL · COMPARATIVE · SEQUENTIAL · CAUSAL · EVALUATIVE · CATEGORICAL

EMPLOY THE SIX
Basic Writing Structures

{Use the basic writing structures to order ideas.}

WRITING IS VERY MUCH ABOUT THE ORDER OF IDEAS presented and the emphasis given to them. In terms of order, we expect ideas to unfold logically, which typically means seeing the most important ideas first. In terms of emphasis, we expect the most important ideas to get the most coverage. The six commonly used structures in writing include: (1) categorical (2) evaluative (3) chronological (4) comparative (5) sequential, and (6) causal. The emphasis or weight given to ideas is important in all structures. The more you write about something, the more important that idea or topic is deemed to be. Order is also important, but not of paramount importance, in all cases. Structures in which order is of importance include chronological, comparative, sequential, and causal structures.

In chronological structures, you discuss the earliest events first and move forward in time. In comparative structures, the most important ideas come before any others. In sequential structures, you begin with the first item in a sequence and end with the last item in the sequence. In cause-and-effect structures, causes are usually identified and discussed before their effects.

In other structures, order is less important. These include categorical and evaluative structures. If we choose to structure our writing by category, it will not make much difference whether we talk about America, China, and then Britain, or start with Britain, go onto China, and finish with America. The same is true with structures based on evaluation; it generally makes little difference whether we discuss pros first (and cons second) or pros last (and cons first).

Although not considered classic writing structures, two other common writing formats include "Question and Answer" and "Problem and Solution." These structures tend to be less formal, and are often used with memos, handouts, and flyers.

> *NOTE* ☞ Writing structures relate to the body of a writing piece, not the introduction or conclusion.

Zoology Rule 101: You can tell by looking at the skeleton what kind of an animal it is.

SUMMARY OF THE SIX WRITING STRUCTURES

	STRUCTURE	PROPER ORDER	EXAMPLES
1	**Categorical** • Item 1, item 2, item 3 • A, B or B, A • A, B, C or C, B, A	• Discuss items in any order.	**2 items** • Let's talk about apples and oranges. **3 items** • Let's talk about America, China, and Britain.
2	**Evaluative** • Pros and cons • Positives and negatives • Pluses and minuses	• Discuss the pro-side first, then the con-side, then the neutral side (if applicable).	**2 items** • Let's talk about the weather: sunny but humid. **3 items** • Let's talk about what voters think: those for, those against, and those undecided.
3	**Chronological** • Past, present, future • Before, during, after	• Discuss early events first, followed by later events.	**2 items** • Let's talk about sales from March to May. **3 items** • Let's talk about Europe's economy: 1800s, 1900s, and the year 2000 and beyond.

	STRUCTURE	PROPER ORDER	EXAMPLES
4	**Comparative** • A > B; B > A • C > B > A • C > A or B	• Discuss most relevant contrasting features first; discuss less important features next.	**2 items** • Let's discuss our most important goals and our minor goals. **3 items** • Let's compare our company to our competitors: size, products, and people and resources
5	**Sequential** • 1st, 2nd, 3rd • X to Y to Z (or reverse)	• Discuss items in order of sequence, from first to last (or in reverse)	**2 items** • Let's discuss drug addiction that progresses from soft drugs to hard drugs. **3 items** • Let's talk about lawmaking at the municipal, state, and national levels.
6	**Causal** • A leads to B • A and B lead to C • A⟶B • A + B⟶C	• Discuss causes before effects.	**2 items** • Let's talk about whether the increase in unemployment is the cause of the increase in crime. **3 items** • Let's talk about the primary causes of global warming, the likely effects of global warming, and the controversy surrounding the issue.

WRITING STRUCTURE OUTLINES

These are sample outlines highlighting the six types of writing structures.

CATEGORICAL

Introduction

Let's discuss three countries.

America ...

China ...

Britain ...

Conclusion

EVALUATIVE

Introduction

Let's evaluate what voters think.

Those for our party ...

Those against our party ...

Those still undecided ...

Conclusion

CHRONOLOGICAL

Introduction

Let's discuss the economy of Europe.

In the 1800s ...

In the 1900s ...

In the year 2000 and beyond ...

Conclusion

SEQUENTIAL

Introduction

Let's discuss law-making hierarchy at three levels.

At the municipal level ...

At the state level ...

At the national level ...

Conclusion

COMPARATIVE

Introduction

Let's compare our company to our competitors.

In terms of size ...

In terms of products and services ...

In terms of people and resources ...

Conclusion

CAUSAL

Introduction

Let's discuss the primary causes and likely effects of global warming.

The primary causes are ...

The likely effects are ...

The controversy is ...

Conclusion

Below are two representative samples of "Question and Answer" and "Problem and Solution" formats. One you might find as part of a travel brochure; the other you might find as part of a business memo.

QUESTION AND ANSWER EXAMPLE

Question: *What is the best way to visit another country?*
Answer: *Take only pictures and leave only footprints.*

Question: *How can we help protect endangered animals?*
Answer: *Fight against loss of animal habitat, prosecute poachers, and prohibit the sale or purchase of endangered animals and their by-products.*

PROBLEM AND SOLUTION EXAMPLE

During our annual conference, many corporate issues were raised. Here is a list of problems cited and our proposed solution.

Problem: *High employee turnover.*
Solution: *Put more effort into recruiting; establish an in-house training program; institute weekly happy hours each Friday, paid for by the company.*

Problem: *Increased marketplace competition.*
Solution: *Redefine our company focus; discontinue products and product lines which fail the 80-20 rule; hold employee brainstorming sessions in hopes of finding new ideas and creative solutions.*

KEEP LIKE
Things Together

{Finish discussing one topic before going on to discuss other topics.}

IMAGINE VISITING THE ZOO TO FIND THAT ALL OF the animals are in one big cage. It would be not only dangerous for the animals, but also nearly impossible for visitors to view the animals in any coherent manner. Sometimes a written work can be, unfortunately, like a zoo, in which all of the different animals (ideas) are in one big cage, running wild. The ideas we describe when we write (as when we speak) should be grouped together. It is best to finish discussing one idea before going on to discuss another.

Here's an example of an essay with jumbled ideas.

ORIGINAL VERSION

In 1981, Roger Sperry received the Nobel Prize for his proof of the split-brain theory. According to Dr. Sperry, the brain has two hemispheres with different, but overlapping functions.

The left side of the brain is responsible for analytical, linear, verbal, and rational thought. Left-brain thinking is "spotlight" thinking. The right hemisphere is holistic, imaginative, nonverbal, and artistic. It is the left brain that a person relies on when balancing a checkbook, remembering names and dates, or setting goals and objectives. Whenever a person recalls another person's face, becomes engrossed in a symphony, or simply daydreams, that person is engaging in right-brain functions. Right-brain thinking is "floodlight" thinking and right-brain processes are, to the chagrin of many, less often rewarded in school. Since most of the Western concepts of thinking come from Greek logic, which is a linear logic system, left-brained processes are most rewarded in the Western education system.

In summary, the right and left hemispheres of the brain each specialize in distinct types of thinking processes. In the most basic sense, the left brain is the analytical side while the right brain is the creative side.

Note that although the structure above is classic, containing an introduction, body, and conclusion, the content is more difficult to read and absorb because ideas are tangled. If this discussion were to continue for a couple of pages, the reader's mind might feel like spaghetti. We know that there are two things under discussion—left-brain vs. right-brain thinking—but the technique with which ideas are described, supported, and impacted is deficient.

CORRECTED VERSION 1

In 1981, Roger Sperry received the Nobel Prize for his proof of the split-brain theory. According to Dr. Sperry, the brain has two hemispheres with different, but overlapping functions. The right and left hemispheres of the brain each specialize in distinct types of thinking processes. In the most basic sense, the left brain is the analytical side while the right brain is the creative side.

The left side of the brain is responsible for analytical, linear, verbal, and rational thought. It is the left brain that a person relies on when balancing a checkbook, remembering names and dates, or setting goals and objectives. The right hemisphere is holistic, imaginative, nonverbal, and artistic. Whenever a person recalls another person's face, becomes engrossed in a symphony, or simply daydreams, that person is engaging in right-brain functions.

Right-brain thinking is characterized as "floodlight" thinking and left-brain thinking as "spotlight" thinking. Since most of the Western concepts of thinking are derived from Greek logic, which is a linear logic system, left-brained processes are most rewarded in the Western education system; right-brain processes are, to the chagrin of many, less often rewarded in school.

In the corrected example, we also have classic usage of introduction, body, and conclusion. The structure in the second paragraph proceeds as follows: left-brain thinking is described first (in one sentence) followed by a one sentence example of left-brain thinking. Then right-brain thinking is described (in one sentence) followed by a one sentence example of right-brain thinking. The first sentence of the third paragraph proceeds with another summary of left-brain vs. right-brain thinking, then concludes with an implication of the two types of thinking.

CORRECTED VERSION 2

> *In 1981, Roger Sperry received the Nobel Prize for his proof of the split-brain theory. According to Dr. Sperry, the brain has two hemispheres with different, but overlapping functions. The right and left hemispheres of the brain each specialize in distinct types of thinking processes. In the most basic sense, the left brain is the analytical side while the right brain is the creative side.*
>
> *The left side of the brain is responsible for analytical, linear, verbal, and rational thought. Left-brain thinking is "spotlight" thinking; it is the left brain that a person relies on when balancing a checkbook, remembering names and dates, or setting goals and objectives. Since most of the Western concepts of thinking are derived from Greek logic, which is a linear logic system, left-brained processes are most rewarded in the Western education system.*
>
> *The right hemisphere is holistic, imaginative, nonverbal, and artistic. Whenever a person recalls another person's face, becomes engrossed in a symphony, or simply daydreams, that person is engaging in right-brain functions. Right-brain thinking is "floodlight" thinking but, to the chagrin of many, these processes are less often rewarded in school.*

The structure in this version is divided entirely between left- and right-brain thinking. In the second paragraph, left-brain thinking is described first (in one sentence) followed by both a one sentence example of left-brain thinking and a one sentence implication of left-brain thinking. In the third paragraph, right-brain thinking is described (in one sentence) followed also by a one sentence example of right-brain thinking and a one sentence implication of right-brain thinking. In short, Corrected Versions 1 and 2 are superior to the Original Version because they do a better job of grouping and contrasting ideas.

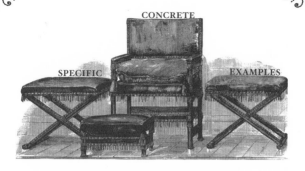

SUPPORT
What You Say

{Use specific and concrete words to support what you say.}

ONE MAJOR DIFFERENCE BETWEEN GOOD WRITING AND mediocre writing lies with the specific and concrete examples that you use or fail to use. Say, for example, you are writing about an apple. Not all apples are identical. What kind of apple is it? Golden Delicious, Granny Smith, Jonathan? What color is it? What shape is it? How does it taste? What is its texture? Where is it grown? Let's look at an example in a business context. Suppose you hear that your company's profits are down. What are the specifics?

Did the sales volume decline? Was the sales price reduced? Did costs go up? And, if any of the above, then by how much? Note the difference in each of the following statements:

GENERAL BUT NOT SPECIFIC

Corporate profits decreased.

GENERAL BUT STILL NOT SPECIFIC

Corporate profits decreased because costs increased.

SPECIFIC

Corporate profits decreased by 10 percent as overall costs increased by 20 percent.

EVEN BETTER

Corporate profits decreased by 10 percent as overall costs increased by 20 percent. In particular, higher salary expenses were the major reason for the increase in costs. Higher salary costs were primarily the result of increases in executive compensation; the aggregate wages paid to factory workers actually decreased by 5 percent due to a decrease in the number of overtime hours clocked.

Examples and details are the very things people remember long after reading a piece. Compare the two examples below describing the popular attitude toward science.

VERSION 1

The popular attitude toward science in the United States is a mix of superstition and awe. Quaint folklore portrays scientific genius as solitary and requiring no nurture. Within the public imagination, such pleasant thoughts go undisturbed by the reality of today's gigantic research labs.

VERSION 2

The popular attitude toward science in the United States is a mix of superstition and awe. Quaint folklore portrays scientific genius as solitary and requiring no nurture. Within the public imagination are visions of the Wright Brothers at work in their bicycle shop, contriving the first flying machine, and of Thomas Edison plumbing the mysteries of electricity with a few magnets and some pieces of wire. Such pleasant thoughts go undisturbed by the reality of today's gigantic research labs.

The second version uses examples drawn from the Wright Brothers and Thomas Edison. This helps us visualize what the author is saying.

Consider the two memos below. Which one would convince you to attend the Calgary Stampede and Exhibition?

MEMO 1

The Calgary Stampede will be held during the first week of July. There will be loads of activities, fun, and food for all. Bring your cowboy hat and boots. See you there!

MEMO 2

The Calgary Stampede will be held during the first week of July. The exhibition grounds are home to two dozen midway rides, a myriad of food stalls (try those miniature doughnuts!), the sounds of live country music, native Indian exhibits, bustling saloons, and a large casino. For the young-sters, there is a petting zoo, magic tricks, and loads of games, with the chance to win giant stuffed animals. The opening day parade has a flotilla of floats, and daily rodeo events include calf roping, bull riding, and chuck wagon races. Fantastic fireworks each evening. See you there!

Note that the second and better example is longer than the original. There may be a question as to why the shorter example is not better because writing should be concise. A trade-off exists between brevity and detail. Sufficient detail will make a piece of writing longer, but this does not necessarily indicate wordiness. Conciseness requires a minimum number of words at the sentence level, whereas sufficient support may require more sentences.

Here is a more humorous example. Consider which of the following better proves to you that a book is a wonderful tool.

BLURB 1

Books are marvelous tools. They're informative and entertaining, and they are here to stay.

BLURB 2

The book is a revolutionary breakthrough in modern technology. No wires, no circuits, no batteries. Nothing to be connected or switched on. It's so easy, even a child can operate it. Just lift its cover! Compact and portable, it can be used anywhere—even sitting in an armchair by the fire. Yet it is powerful enough to hold as much information as a CD.

This is how it works: The book may be picked up at any time and used by merely opening it. The book never crashes and never needs rebooting. The browse feature allows you to move instantly to any sheet, and move forward or backward as you wish. Many come with an index feature, which pinpoints the exact location of selected information for instant retrieval. You can also make personal notes next to book entries with an optional programming tool, the Portable Erasable Nib Cryptic Intercommunication Language Stylus (PENCILS).

Is this the end of the computer? The BOOK (Built in Orderly Organized Knowledge) looks as though it will become the entertainment wave of the future.

Vague language weakens your writing because it forces the reader to guess at what you mean instead of allowing the reader to concentrate fully on your ideas and style. Choose specific, descriptive words for more forceful writing. Sometimes, to be specific and concrete, you will have to use more words than usual. That's okay. While it is important to cut unnecessary words, it is equally important to properly support what you say.

Exercises

Rewrite the following sentences to replace vague language with specific, concrete language. Suggested answers are on pages 145-146.

1. Joannie has a dog and a cat.
2. The vacation was expensive.
3. Amanda is a careless person.
4. Many economists think that the Federal Reserve Bank is to blame for the current economic downturn.
5. Firms should advertise because advertising will surely increase sales.
6. Sheila is tall and good-looking.
7. Rainbows are colorful.
8. The student was unable to complete the assignment as required.
9. The store is packed with goods.
10. Mr. and Mrs. Jones make a good couple.

TRAIN YOURSELF TO CITE SPECIFIC EXAMPLES

Most writing suffers from superficiality—it is too general. Examples abound in both the academic and professional realm. For example, when writing job search letters or college application essays, candidates often write sentences such as "I have good people skills," "I have good communication skills," or "I have good analytical skills."

There is a debater's adage: "A statement without support merits a denial without reason." If one person says, "Purple polka-dot bikinis are awful" but gives no evidence to support the statement, another person is entitled to say, "You're wrong," and not give a reason. A valued technique, which can be used when writing rough drafts, is to stress the points you wish to make by placing "for example" immediately after what you write. This will ensure that you lend support to your statements.

> *NOTE* ✒ As a matter of practicality, each writer should decide whether to leave "for example" in an essay or to edit it out, particularly if looking for a more seamless connection between ideas and support points.

The following sample sentences were taken directly from the essays of applicants applying to college or graduate school.

EXAMPLE 1

Candidate's statement:

> *I am an energetic, loyal, creative, diligent, honest, strict, humorous, responsible, flexible, and ambitious person.*

Reviewer's likely comment:

> *Do you care to develop your discussion and support a few of these traits with concrete examples?*

A real amateur's mistake is to use a shopping list of traits to describe someone. This problem usually emerges when writing a personal essay. It can also arise when requesting other people to write about you, as is the case when writing academic or professional letters of recommendation or job reference letters. Giving adequate support for a dozen traits is practically impossible. The better approach is to choose two or three traits and develop each in more detail.

EXAMPLE 2

Candidate's statement:

> *Growing up in both the East and West, I have experienced both Asian and Western points of view.*

Reviewer's likely comment:

> *What are these Asian and Western points of view?*

EXAMPLE 3

Candidate's statement:

> *Although ABC Company did not flourish, I still consider my effort a success because I was able to identify strengths and weaknesses in my overall business skills.*

Reviewer's likely comment:

> *What strengths and weaknesses did you identify?*

EXAMPLE 4

Candidate's statement:

> *Not only did I develop important operational skills in running a business, but I experienced and witnessed the challenges that entrepreneurs face on a daily basis.*

Reviewer's likely comment:

What were these challenges?

The following examples show how unsupported statements can be improved with the addition of concrete details.

ORIGINAL

I was brought up out of context—an English girl in a British colony. I went through thirteen years of international school and my primary school had twenty-eight nationalities.

BETTER

I was brought up out of context—an English girl in a British colony. I went through thirteen years of international school and my primary school had twenty-eight nationalities. I remember when my fourth-year teacher decided to hold an International Day. Everyone wore a traditional or national costume and brought a dish of traditional cuisine. There is no real national costume for England, so I dressed as an English Rose, and brought Yorkshire Parkin, a sweet ginger cake, as my dish.

ORIGINAL

I grew up in a Maine farm family that was ethnically Scottish, but really your everyday New England household. I am thankful now for a stable, happy childhood. My parents gave me the best education and upbringing they could. They taught me to be caring and respectful of people and the environment. They taught me honesty, humility, and the silliness of pretense.

BETTER

I grew up in a Maine farm family that was ethnically Scottish, but really your everyday New England household. I am thankful now for a stable, happy childhood. My parents gave me the best education and upbringing they could. They took me to museums, libraries, and ballet lessons. They taught me to be caring and respectful of people and the environment. Often they taught by example: When I was four or five, my elder brothers and I accidentally lit a field on fire. Wind caught the flames and quickly it engulfed the field and came dangerously close to our house and barn. After the fire was put out, my parents felt our guilt and remorse and never mentioned it. We learned the mercy of compassion and forgiveness in addition to the foolishness of playing with matches in dry fields on windy days. My mother taught me honesty in a different way: When we stole balloons, she made us return them and individually admit our guilt, apologize, and offer to pay from our birthday money (we didn't get allowances). The humility of facing that storekeeper (whose sweet disposition and insistence that we keep the balloons made my guilt worse) has stayed with me until this day.

WEAKNESSES IN SUPPORT TECHNIQUES

The next two examples are letters of recommendation, as frequently seen in the graduate school application process, and a job reference letter. A critique of both letters follows. In short, like so many academic and business documents, these letters could be made effective if more specific support was given in the form of examples, quotes, or anecdotes. In writing parlance, don't just mention the "what's", mention the "so what's". Mentioning the "so what's" provides support and indicates the reason why the writer is writing about something.

ACADEMIC LETTER OF RECOMMENDATION

Admissions Director:

It is my pleasure to serve as a reference for Richard Tyler in his application for admission to your graduate school. I have known Richard for fourteen years, first as an associate of his father (we worked together in a large U.S. conglomerate from 1994 to 2001). Later Richard worked for me at Xerox Corporation as an accountant and financial analyst.

Richard demonstrated a high level of intelligence, strong technical skills, and a very effective and positive way of interacting with people. He gained quickly the respect and support of his peers and seniors. He made a substantial contribution at Xerox Corporation during his period of service. I would particularly like to cite his originality and desire to innovate new systems and procedures.

Another remarkable quality worthy of mention is Richard's wide range of interests—from the specific and exacting profession of accounting and quantitative analysis to the broad interests that took him to Japan for study and international experience. This is a unique range.

Based on my 32-year career in the financial management of hi-tech companies, my own graduate school degree, and knowledge of many applicants and young graduates over the years, I would rank Richard in the top 10 percent of his peers now applying for admission.

Sincerely,

Frank B. Moore Jr.
VP Finance and Chief Financial Officer
Xerox Systems of America

JOB REFERENCE LETTER

To Whom It May Concern:

As a sales representative at the newly opened branch of Avon Cosmetic Products in Hong Kong, Judith was initially responsible for attending to the phones and walk-in customers. This was a new center for Avon International, and women's accessories was a brand new product area for the Hong Kong and PRC customers. Judith not only exceeded her sales quotas but also became our regional expert on how to adapt, modify, and package all our local products.

Besides having a very special organizational ability, Judith also has a wonderful way with her co-workers and customers. Co-workers listen to her advice and customers continue to buy from her. We have all watched Judith develop her marketing and sales skills. If she were not planning on leaving to go overseas, we would have offered her the position of being the director of our Beijing Avon Office, where she would not only administrate, but also train sales staff to open the China market.

As the person who started the Avon Hong Kong Office and hired Judith, I am most proud of finding her for our company. She is extremely talented, diligent, and innovative, and all without formal business training. We sorely hate to lose her. I have never met another person who has greater potential to be a truly great marketer. Thus, I unqualifiedly and enthusiastically write this job reference letter. Your company will be proud of such an employee.

Sincerely,

Elizabeth Lee
Director, Avon Cosmetics (Hong Kong) Ltd.

CRITIQUE OF RECOMMENDATION LETTER

This recommendation (or appraisal) letter follows a traditional format for a graduate school letter of recommendation. It cites at a minimum the context in which the recommender knows the candidate, and a quantifiable comparison is made of the candidate to others applying to graduate school. This letter constitutes a solid endorsement; the only criticism is that it misses a few opportunities to cite details in support of things said. For example, the reviewer is likely to respond to the recommender's statement, "I would particularly like to cite his originality and desire to innovate new systems and procedures" by asking for details on these new systems and procedures. Moreover, the best professional recommendations may also make mention of a candidate's career aspirations, as well as areas of needed development. Sometimes the recommender cites anecdotes or quotes that other persons have made about the applicant as additional support.

CRITIQUE OF JOB REFERENCE LETTER

This job reference letter is a positive one, written in a light, colloquial tone. It comes across as warm and personable. A criticism of this letter lies in the lack of concrete details to support the recommender's statements. For example, the reviewer may want to know how much Judith exceeded her sales quota—by 1 percent or 200 percent—as well as the growth in sales of the Hong Kong office and how much of it should be credited to Judith's efforts. The recommender should give one example of how Judith adapted, modified, or packaged new products for the local market because the reviewer is no doubt interested. Perhaps the recommender could quote one of Judith's customers. Finally, the letter should mention one area where Judith is weak, to balance out the recommendation.

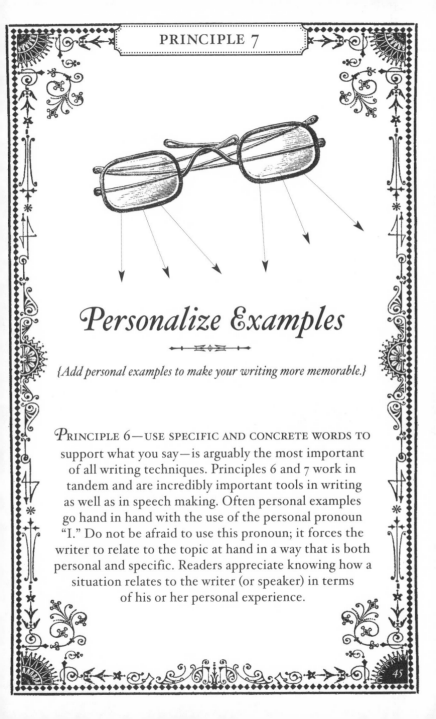

Personalize Examples

{Add personal examples to make your writing more memorable.}

PRINCIPLE 6—USE SPECIFIC AND CONCRETE WORDS TO support what you say—is arguably the most important of all writing techniques. Principles 6 and 7 work in tandem and are incredibly important tools in writing as well as in speech making. Often personal examples go hand in hand with the use of the personal pronoun "I." Do not be afraid to use this pronoun; it forces the writer to relate to the topic at hand in a way that is both personal and specific. Readers appreciate knowing how a situation relates to the writer (or speaker) in terms of his or her personal experience.

For example, the statement "Nigel is too busy to enjoy himself" is a general statement. The statement "Despite working evenings, Nigel arrives home and diligently tackles his homework to prepare for next day's classes" is a personal statement that makes the same point.

Personalizing examples makes them more memorable. The following examples will give you some idea of how to use generic and detailed support points. Detailed support points give the reader an idea of what the writer personally came away with as a result of such and such experience.

> *NOTE* ☞ When writing formal or academic reports, the use of the personal pronoun "I" should generally be avoided.

STATEMENT

> *I have analytical skills.*

GENERIC SUPPORT POINT

> *Analytical skills help me work with numbers to both read and interpret financial statements. Analytical skills serve as objective measures and as the basis of good decision making.*

DETAILED SUPPORT POINT

> *My time spent working at Andersen Consulting helped me develop an analytical mindset. I learned to reconcile what was said verbally with its financial reality. When a client said his or her problem was high costs, I systematically broke down total costs into their individual components. Once I knew where the numbers pointed, I looked for the stories behind these numbers. Sometimes the problem was not with high costs as the client may have thought, but with another factor in the overall system.*

STATEMENT

People are starving.

GENERIC SUPPORT POINT

People are starving—you can see it in their eyes and in the way their bones press against their skin.

DETAILED SUPPORT POINT

But it's the faces you can't forget, like images in a recurring nightmare, they keep coming back, haunted faces, staring blankly back from the windows of tumble-down hovels. The hollow lifeless eyes, skin stretched tight across backs, hands outstretched, dull listless eyes imploring. I move as if in a dream through the agony that is famine.

The above is an excerpt from the movie *The Year of Living Dangerously*, depicting the experiences of a young journalist stationed in Indonesia in the mid-1960s. This detailed support point also mimics the time-honored writer's adage "show, don't tell." Writing at an emotional level helps ensure that the reader gets a firsthand account, not a secondhand one.

Another potential weakness in support techniques occurs when students present records of extracurricular involvement when applying to college or graduate school. Because of the intense competition for entrance to highly rated schools, a candidate should present solid support for his or her involvement. Applicants often fall short, only mentioning the names of their extracurricular activities and the hours of involvement. Notice how much more meaningful a presentation becomes when a candidate not only provides proper support for what is being said, but also personalizes the writing by providing a detailed support point.

PRESENTATION OF A HIGH SCHOOL EXTRACURRICULAR ACTIVITY

Varsity Debate Team Member
Arizona High School
Sept 2002 to May 2003

Time
Seven to ten hours per week excluding library research and occasional weekend travel

Description
Competed in high school NDT debate and participated in individual speaking events; won two regional debate tournaments, Pomona Invitational and West Coast Challenge.

Summary
Debate taught me four things:
• to organize and defend coherent arguments
• to speak under pressure
• to develop excellent research skills
• to formulate strategies for beating tournament competitors

My time spent in debate taught me to develop affirmative and negative briefs to support and defend the resolution at hand. I learned to be ever mindful of the importance of anticipating both sides of an argument. For every argument there is an equal and opposite argument. It is here that I gained my first real insights into an old tenet of philosophy: "Only through contrast do we have awareness."

Literary techniques also can be used to strengthen your personal or even business writing. Think of these writing techniques as optional tools to support the things you say in addition to examples and statistics.

ANECDOTES

Anecdotes are little stories used to embellish your point. For example, suppose you are writing about why we should follow our own path and not be unduly persuaded by the advice of others. You write:

> *This situation reminds me of the story of a young violinist who is fraught with the dilemma of whether she possesses the talent to continue playing the violin and reach her lofty goal of becoming a virtuoso. Upon a fortuitous meeting with a master violinist, the young girl asks, "Will you listen to me play and tell me if you think I have the talent to be a virtuoso?" The master then responds, "If I listen to you play, and I feel you do not have the talent, what will you do?" The girl replies, "Since I value highly your opinion, I will stop playing." The master remarks, "If you would quit because of what I would say, then you obviously do not have what it takes to be a virtuoso."*

QUOTATIONS

Including quotations, particularly those attributed to famous or well-known people, can be a persuasive tool. Quotations, when well chosen, make you look intelligent. Unfortunately, it is not always easy to recall an applicable quote from memory and a little research will likely be needed. In addition to numerous quotation books available, try using an Internet search engine.

ANALOGIES

Analogies draw similarities between two otherwise dissimilar things and help the reader see a given relationship more clearly. For example, suppose you are writing an essay and want to stress the importance of making sales, particularly the relationship between the production department and the sales and marketing department. You might use the following "guns and bullets" analogy: "Production makes the bullets, marketing points the gun, and sales pulls the trigger." This makes clearer the idea that the production department is responsible for making products while the marketing department is responsible for determining where sales are to be found, and the sales department for actually going out and making sales.

Say for example you wish to use an analogy to describe the difference between a person's personality and his or her mood swings. A climate versus weather analogy might be appropriate, such as "Climate is like our fundamental personality traits while weather is like our emotions and moods."

SIMILES AND METAPHORS

Similes compare two unlike things and are usually introduced by "like" or "as." An example of a simile is "A sharp mind is like a knife that cuts problems open." Similes are relatively easy to use and can be powerful tools in presenting your ideas.

Metaphors literally denote that one thing is another (instead of one thing being like another), and the words "as" or "like" are not used. An example of a metaphor is "He has nerves of steel."

Similes and metaphors are figurative comparisons, not actual comparisons. An example of an actual comparison is "Cindy is taller than Susan." Even though the focus of this book is on expository writing, and the use of analogies, similes, and metaphors present techniques which touch on creative writing, there are still uses for such literary techniques in everyday writing.

Sales letters provide an everyday business example where the use of creativity is used to grab the reader's attention. Ponder these opening liners.

A motivational or human resource company begins a sales letter with a simile: "Without a goal, a person is like a ship without a rudder."

A wine distributor advertises (by analogy): "Good wine and a good physician have one thing in common. They both can help extend your life!"

A bungee jump operator employs a metaphor: "Do you have the heart of a lion?"

Exercise

Try answering the following question:

> *How is a good idea like an iceberg?*

Reflect on the statement above and write several one-sentence responses. Rest assured that by coming up with a half-dozen answers to this difficult example above, you will find crafting others for everyday writing purposes just that much easier. Possible answers are listed on page 146.

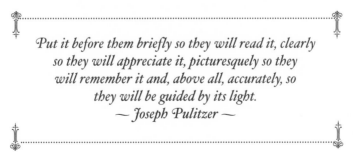

Put it before them briefly so they will read it, clearly so they will appreciate it, picturesquely so they will remember it and, above all, accurately, so they will be guided by its light.
— Joseph Pulitzer —

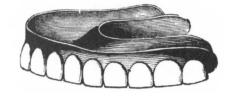

KEEP
It Simple

{Use simple words to express your ideas.}

THE MOST FUNDAMENTAL WAY TO SIMPLIFY WRITING IS to use simpler words. Simpler words—verbs, nouns, and adjectives—have broader meanings in English while more complicated words have more specific meanings. Thus, you have a higher margin for error when using simpler words. The following chart shows how we may substitute a less familiar word with a more familiar, and therefore, more understandable word.

USING SIMPLER WORDS

Acceded	— Agreed	Execute	— Carry out
Accommodate	— Serve	Expedite	— Rush
Accumulate	— Gather	Explicit	— Stated
Adaptability	— Adapt	Facilitate	— Make easy
Affirmative	— Yes	Generate	— Produce
Aggregate	— Total	Implementation	— Implement
Ameliorate	— Improve	Maintenance	— Upkeep
Ascertain	— Learn	Materialize	— Develop
Cognizant	— Aware	Modification	— Change
Compel	— Force	Notwithstanding	— Despite
Compensate	— Pay	Optimum	— Best
Concerning	— About	Preparatory	— Planned
Demonstrate	— Show	Procure	— Obtain, Buy
Determine	— Find	Proficiency	— Skill
Distribute	— Give	Replacements	— Replace
Effect	— Make	Resourcefulness	— Resourceful
Encounter	— Meeting	Standardization	— Standardize
Endeavor	— Try	Utilize	— Use

NOTE ❦ Some writers adhere to the idea that "big words" are bad. The belief is that anyone who uses big words is just trying to impress the reader. The point embodied by Principle 8 is that the everyday writer should err on the side of using simpler words. That is not to say that there is no occasion for "bigger" or more specific vocabulary in writing, but rather that the writer should always consider how appropriate the writing is for a given audience.

Exercises

Rewrite the following sentences by expressing the ideas more simply. The suggested answers are on page 147.

1. There is considerable evidential support for the assertion that carrot juice is good for you.
2. We anticipate utilizing hundreds of reams of copy paper in the foreseeable future.
3. This plan will provide for the elimination of inefficient business practices.
4. Educationwise, our schoolchildren should be given adequate training in the three Rs—reading, writing, and arithmetic.
5. Only meteorologists can perform a detailed analysis of changing climatic conditions.
6. With reference to the poem, I submit that the second and third stanzas connote a certain despair.
7. That dog is the epitome, the very quintessence, of canine excellence.
8. The hurricane destroyed almost all structures along the coastline. Most homes were destroyed when water and wind joined forces to rip off roofs and collapse walls.
9. Which point of view do I adhere to? That's a good question. While I am against war, I also realize that some situations require the use of military force.
10. Like Napoleon's army that marched on Russia more than a century before, the German army was also unable to successfully invade Russia because its soldiers were inadequately prepared for winter conditions. German soldiers didn't even have proper winter clothing to withstand the subzero temperatures.

CUT DOWN
Long Sentences

{Make your writing clearer by dividing up long sentences.}

O NE WAY TO MAKE YOUR WRITING CLEARER IS TO LIMIT the use of long sentences. The easiest way to do this is to divide a long sentence into two or more shorter sentences. Caveat: The practice of using short sentences does not mean that all sentences should be short. This would create a choppy style and is precisely where the art of writing comes into play. The writer must judge how to weave short sentences with longer ones, as well as how to use sentence variety. (See Principle 14.)

Here's an example of a very long sentence that needs help.

ORIGINAL

Leadership—whether on the battlefield or in another area, such as politics or business—can take place either by example or command, and Alexander the Great, renowned in both history and legend, is a good example of a military leader who led by both command and personal example, whereas Gandhi and Mother Teresa, both famous for their devotion to great causes, provide instances of people leading primarily by the power of inspiring personal example.

Cutting this large sentence into at least two or three smaller sentences would result in the following:

BETTER

Leadership can take place either by example or command. Alexander the Great is an example of a military leader who did both. Gandhi and Mother Teresa, on the other hand, led primarily by the power of inspiring personal example.

Here is another example of a "one-sentence paragraph":

I entered the Neurological Faculty of the hospital and endured the next three months undergoing various diagnostic tests including EEG monitoring in which my brain's electrical rhythms were monitored by electrodes placed on my scalp held by adhesive glue to record activity over a period of time, daily blood testing and blood counts, and all the required tests which subjected my brain to further diagnostic imaging from CAT scanning (computerized tomography), to an MRI (magnetic resonance imaging), to the costly PET scanning and even the painful spinal fluid testing.

Obviously the previous sentence is running wild. Cut this large sentence into two or three smaller sentences, as follows:

BETTER

> *I entered the Neurological Faculty of the hospital and endured three months of diagnostic tests including EEG monitoring, daily blood testing, and blood counts. EEG monitoring subjected my brain to electrical rhythms after electrodes were attached to my scalp. Other diagnostic tests further scrutinized my brain: CAT scans (computerized tomography), MRIs (magnetic resonance imaging), costly PET scans, and even painful spinal fluid testing.*

There is power in short sentences, and their use should not be underestimated. Really short sentences (three to five words) catch the reader's eye and stand out as if naked. Their occasional use can add a dynamic touch to your writing. For example:

> *I like beer. Beer explains more about me than anything in the world. Who am I? I am the beer man, at least that is what many of my close friends call me.*

One idea that carries merit is the *topic sentence, one-line rule*. Topic sentences should ideally not be longer than one line to ensure that the reader grasps your point quickly.

Speaking of beer and bare-naked sentences, the following sentences were used as part of a major campaign for dark beer:

> *Dark is different. Dark is exquisite. Dark is discerning. Dark is determined. Dark is mysterious. Dark is sensual. Dark is smooth. Dark is the other side of one's desire.*

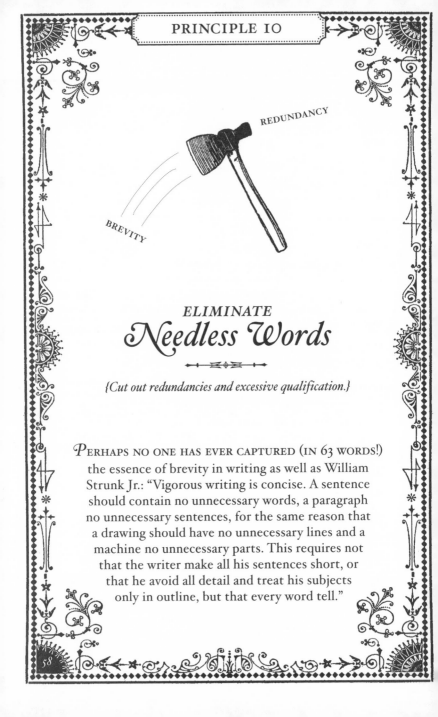

REDUNDANCY

BREVITY

ELIMINATE *Needless Words*

{Cut out redundancies and excessive qualification.}

$\mathcal{P}$ERHAPS NO ONE HAS EVER CAPTURED (IN 63 WORDS!) the essence of brevity in writing as well as William Strunk Jr.: "Vigorous writing is concise. A sentence should contain no unnecessary words, a paragraph no unnecessary sentences, for the same reason that a drawing should have no unnecessary lines and a machine no unnecessary parts. This requires not that the writer make all his sentences short, or that he avoid all detail and treat his subjects only in outline, but that every word tell."

REDUNDANCIES

Redundancy occurs when a writer needlessly repeats a word or an idea. It is redundant to speak of a "beginner lacking experience." The word "beginner" by itself implies lack of experience. Redundant words or phrases can be eliminated without changing the meaning of the sentence.

Redundant	Better
advance notice	— notice
any and all	— any
ask the question	— question
attractive in appearance	— attractive
big in size	— big
blue in color/blue colored	— blue
charming in character	— charming
combined together	— combined
completely full	— full
consensus of opinion	— consensus
continues to remain	— continues or remains
curious in nature	— curious
descend down	— descend
deliberately chosen	— chosen
end result	— result
exceptionally outstanding	— exceptional
few in number	— few
final outcome	— outcome
hope and trust	— hope or trust

if and when	— if
lose out	— lose
may perhaps	— may *or* perhaps
modern world of today	— modern world
mutual agreement	— agreement
new initiatives	— initiatives
new innovation	— innovation
past experience	— experience
past history	— history
positive benefits	— benefits
reiterate again	— reiterate
reflect back	— reflect
repeat (over) again	— repeat
return back	— return
sadly tragic	— tragic
serious crisis	— crisis
sink down	— sink
tall in height	— tall
true facts	— facts
undergraduate student	— undergraduate
unexpected emergency	— emergency
unique and one-of-a-kind	— unique *or* one-of-kind
unsubstantiated rumors	— rumors
until such a time	— until
whether or not	— whether
young juvenile	— juvenile

EXCESSIVE QUALIFICATION

Occasional use of qualifiers will let the reader know you are reasonable, but using such modifiers too often weakens your writing. Excessive qualification makes you sound hesitant, and adds bulk without adding substance.

ORIGINAL

> *This rather serious leak may possibly shake the very foundations of the intelligence world.*

BETTER

> *This serious leak may shake the foundations of the intelligence world.*

And there is no need to quantify words that are already absolute.

Original	Better
fairly excellent	excellent
truly unique	unique
the very worst	the worst
most favorite	favorite
quite outstanding	outstanding

Look also for opportunities to clean out qualifiers such as *a bit*, *a little*, *highly*, *just*, *kind of*, *mostly*, *pretty*, *quite*, *rather*, *really*, *slightly*, *so*, *still*, *somewhat*, *sort of*. Like *very*, *truly*, and *fairly*, they are all weakeners and are almost always unnecessary.

NEEDLESS SELF-REFERENCE

Avoid such unnecessary phrases as "I believe," "I feel," and "in my opinion." There is usually no need to remind your reader that what you are writing is your opinion.

Exercise 1

Rewrite the following sentences, cutting out redundancies.
Suggested answers are on pages 147-148.

1. Employees should be ready, willing, and able to adhere to the company dress code and not wear casual clothes when more formal attire is required.
2. A construction project that large in size needs an effective manager who can get things done.
3. That Metropolitan museum continues to remain a significant tourist attraction.
4. The ultimate conclusion is that physical and psychological symptoms are intertwined and difficult to separate.
5. The promoter's charisma and charming personality do not mask his poor product or technical knowledge.
6. The recently observed trend of government borrowing may eventually create nations that are poorer and more impoverished than ever before.
7. These events—war, recession, and health concerns—have combined together to create a serious crisis.
8. Those who can find novel solutions to problems are few in number.
9. She has deliberately chosen to work for UNESCO.
10. Negotiation opens up many doors to peaceful settlement.

Exercise 2

Rewrite the following sentences, cutting out excessive qualification. Suggested answers are on pages 148-149.

1. Peter is an exceptionally outstanding student.
2. You yourself are the very best person to decide what you should do with your life.

3. The gas tank is completely empty.
4. Joey seems to be sort of a slow reader.
5. There are very many reasons for the disparity of wealth among the world's nations.
6. Every leader should perhaps use a certain amount of diplomacy before resorting to force.
7. In India, I found about the best food I have ever eaten.
8. She is a fairly excellent pianist.
9. The Hermitage Museum in St. Petersburg is filled with unique, one-of-a-kind paintings.
10. Needless to say, auditors should remain independent of the companies that they audit.

Exercise 3

Rewrite the following sentences, cutting out needless self-reference. Suggested answers are on pages 149-150.

1. The speaker, in my personal opinion, is lost in detail.
2. I feel we ought to pay teachers as much as other professionals such as doctors, lawyers, and engineers.
3. I do not think this argument can be generalized to most economically deprived individuals.
4. My own experience shows me that alcohol is a fine social lubricant.
5. I doubt more people would use the library even if books could be delivered to a person's home for free.
6. Although I am no expert, I do not think that freedom of speech means that someone can scream "fire" in a crowded movie theatre and be held blameless.
7. My guess is that most individuals want to get rich, but many fail simply because they do not set and follow through on their goals.
8. I must emphasize that I am not saying that the opposing argument is without merit.

SUBJECT

OBJECT

VERB

GAIN
Active Power

{Favor active sentences, not passive sentences.}

In general, the active voice is preferred to the passive voice because the active voice is more action oriented. The active voice is both more direct and less verbose, cutting down on the number of needed words. For example, the sentence "I loved Sally" is written in the active voice and contains three words. The sentence, "Sally was loved by me" is written in the passive voice and contains five words.

Passive sentences are less direct not only because they reverse the normal Subject-Verb-Object sentence order, but because they often fail to mention the doer of the action.

Passive	*The problem was discovered yesterday.*
Active	*Our intern discovered the problem yesterday.*
Passive	*The writing of the report was easy.*
Active	*She wrote the report easily.*

Writing students are so often told to avoid the passive voice that it is not hard to see why the mere mention of the passive voice leads some zealots to blurt out "passive bad, active good." It is not, however, categorically correct to say that we should always avoid the passive voice. There are times when the passive voice is effective or even necessary. Consider the following:

Passive   *Today, the computer files were erased.*
(The writer's goal is to hide the perpetrator.)

Active   *Today, Al Smith erased the computer files.*
(The writer's goal is to expose the perpetrator.)

In the examples above, the writer must decide whether he or she would like to expose or hide the doer of the action. Another reason for using the passive voice is variety.

EXAMPLE 1

We sat through the visiting professor's intriguing lecture. The discussion centered on why people with higher I.Q.s and lower E.Q.s usually end up working for people with higher E.Q.s but lower I.Q.s. Afterwards, student questions <u>were</u> entertained.

The passive voice is appropriate when the performer of the action is unknown or unimportant.

EXAMPLE 2

> *The world's largest pearl (6.4 kg) <u>was</u> discovered in the Philippines in 1934.*

The discovery of the pearl is important but the discoverer is either unknown or deemed unimportant.

EXAMPLE 3

> *Millions of barrels of oil <u>were</u> pumped from under the desert sand.*

The extraction of oil is deemed important but the extractor is not.

EXAMPLE 4

> *Joyce Buckingham <u>was</u> awarded a medal by the committee organizers.*

Finally, the passive voice is likely preferred when the receiver of the action is more important than the performer of the action.

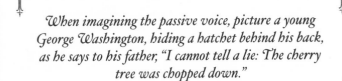

When imagining the passive voice, picture a young George Washington, hiding a hatchet behind his back, as he says to his father, "I cannot tell a lie: The cherry tree was chopped down."

Exercises

Rewrite the following sentences, replacing the passive voice with the active voice. Suggested answers are on page 149-150.

1. In premodern times, medical surgery was often performed by inexperienced and ill-equipped practitioners.
2. The main point made by the author can be found in the last paragraph.
3. Motivational courses are often attended by those who need them least, while they are not sought out by those who have greatest need.
4. The tennis courts must be relocated where they can be used by the apartment residents.
5. Details of the peace agreement were ironed out minutes before the deadline.
6. Red Cross volunteers should be generously praised for their efforts.
7. Book contracts will always be reviewed by an author's literary agent before being signed by the author.
8. Test results were posted with no concern for confidentiality.
9. The report was compiled by a number of clinical psychologists and marriage experts.
10. Without money, staff, and local government support, many diseases in less developed countries cannot be treated.

PRINCIPLE 12

FAVOR VERBS, *Not Nouns*

{Avoid nominalizing your verbs and adjectives.}

THE WORD NOMINALIZATION IS A FANCY SOUNDING
but important concept in writing. It describes the
process by which verbs and adjectives are turned into
nouns. Nominalizations weaken writing for a variety of
reasons, mainly because they make sentences weaker
and usually longer. The next page shows several
examples of nominalizations.

VERBS	NOUNS
reduce	reduction
develop	development
rely	reliability

So, "reduction of costs" is best written as "reduce costs"; "development of a five-year plan" is best written as "develop a five-year plan"; and "reliability of seatbelts" is best written as "rely on seatbelts."

Nominalizations also occur when adjectives are turned into nouns.

ADJECTIVES	NOUNS
precise	precision
creative	creativity
reasonable	reasonableness

So, "precision of measurements" is best written as "precise measurements"; "creativity of individuals" is best written as "creative individuals"; and "reasonable-ness of working hours" is best written as "reasonable working hours."

Also, all verbs can be turned into nouns (called gerunds) when adding *-ing* (e.g., *speaking, carrying,* and *engaging*).

EXAMPLE

> **Original** *Is the drinking of alcohol by students allowed on campus?*

> **Better** *May students drink alcohol on campus?*

The gerund "drinking" is best changed to the verb "drink."

Exercises

Rewrite the following sentences replacing nouns and adjectives with verbs. The answers can be found on pages 150-151.

1. Amateur cyclists must work on the development of their own training programs.
2. The inability to make decisions is a military leader's darkest enemy.
3. The expert panel's best estimate includes a 30 percent reduction in pollution as a result of the implementation of the new clean air bill.
4. Most dietitians advocate cutting out fat and reducing carbohydrates as the best means of losing weight.
5. His reading of the critic's review surprised him.
6. The standardization of entrance exams helps ensure that students can apply to college and graduate school programs on an equal footing.
7. Hearing celebrities airing their political views on television is not in good taste.
8. The applicability of using traditional accounting formulas for the valuation of Internet companies was never seriously questioned by investors until after the dot-com boom.
9. Our supervisor made a decision in favor of terminating those three employees.
10. The difficulty of coursework and the pressure of grading should not discourage students from pursuing new academic ventures.

ALWAYS USE
Parallel Forms

{Express a series of items in consistent, parallel form.}

PARALLELISM IN WRITING MEANS THAT WE SHOULD express similar parts of a sentence in a consistent way. Elements alike in function should be alike in construction. Parallelism builds clarity and power. Note the following sentence in parallel form: "In the summer before college, I waited tables, sold magazines, and even delivered pizzas." Now compare this with a nonparallel form: "In the summer before college, I was a waiter at a restaurant, pursued magazine sales, and even had a stint at delivering pizzas."

Consider the parallelism in the famous quote by former U.S. President John F. Kennedy:

> *Let every nation know, whether it wishes us well or ill, that we shall pay any price, bear any burden, meet any hardship, support any friend, oppose any foe to assure the survival and success of liberty.*

Note how all the verbs are in parallel form. Also, ponder the parallelism of this famous Biblical verse.

> *Blessed are the poor in spirit: for theirs is the kingdom of heaven.*
> *Blessed are they that mourn: for they shall be comforted.*
> *Blessed are the meek: for they shall inherit the earth.*
> *Blessed are they which do hunger and thirst after righteousness: for they shall be filled.*

Parallelism may relate to almost everything—verbs, nouns, pronouns, articles, prepositions, and even adjectives, adverbs, and conjunctions.

Parallelism must be observed closely when we list a series of items. The rule here is that either we repeat the word before every element in a series or include it only before the first item. Anything else violates the rules of parallelism governing a series of items. Your treatment of the second element of the series determines the form of all subsequent elements.

EXAMPLE 1

Original	*They went to London, to Paris, and Istanbul.*
Correct	*They went <u>to</u> London, <u>to</u> Paris, and <u>to</u> Istanbul.*
Or	*They went <u>to</u> London, Paris, and Istanbul.*

EXAMPLE 2

Original   *She likes sun, the sand, and going to the sea.*

Correct   *She likes <u>the</u> sun, <u>the</u> sand, and <u>the</u> sea.*

Or   *She likes <u>the</u> sun, sand, and sea.*

EXAMPLE 3

Original   *The entrepreneur <u>had</u> the personality, the contacts, and <u>had</u> the intelligence to succeed in almost any business venture.*

Correct   *The entrepreneur <u>had</u> the personality, <u>had</u> the contacts, and <u>had</u> the intelligence to succeed in almost any business venture.*

Or   *The entrepreneur <u>had</u> the personality, contacts, and intelligence to succeed in almost any business venture.*

Exercises

Rewrite the following sentences using parallel structure. Suggested answers are on pages 151-152.

1. All business students learn the basics of accounting, marketing fundamentals, and how to do manufacturing.
2. The fund manager based his theory on stock performance, bond performance, and on other leading economic indicators.
3. The witness spoke with seriousness and in a concerned tone.

4. The requirements for a business degree are not as stringent as a medical degree.
5. The dancer taught her understudy how to move, to dress, how to work with choreographers and deal with photographers.
6. The documentary was interesting and replete with pertinent information.
7. The couple invested their money in stocks, bonds, and in a piece of real estate.
8. The painting may be done either in watercolors or with oils.
9. Olympic volunteers were ready, fully able, and were quite determined to do a great job.
10. My objections regarding pending impeachment are, first, the personal nature of the matter; second, that it is partisan.

ELIMINATE UNNECESSARY WORDS

Parallelism also involves rules for when we can acceptably eliminate words in a sentence and still retain clear meaning. The three biggest problem areas occur with verbs, prepositions, and correlative conjunctions. In the case of verbs (or verb forms) and prepositions, it is okay to omit a second verb or preposition if it is the same as the first. To check for faulty parallelism, complete each component idea in a sentence and make sure each part of the sentence can stand alone. For instance, in the sentence "New York City is large and exciting," there is no need to say "New York City is large and is exciting," since the second verb "is" is the same as the first, and needs not be written out.

VERBS

Original *In my favorite Japanese restaurant, the food is fascinating and the drinks expensive.*

Correct   *In my favorite Japanese restaurant, the food <u>is</u> fascinating and the drinks <u>are</u> expensive.*

Original   *Tasmania has and always will be an island.*

Correct   *Tasmania <u>has been</u> and always <u>will be</u> an island.*

NOTE ❧ The verb in the second part of the sentence is different and must be written out.

PREPOSITIONS

Original   *John is interested but not very good at golf.*

Correct   *John is interested <u>in</u> but not very good <u>at</u> golf.*

NOTE ❧ The preposition in the second part of the sentence is different and must be written out.

CORRELATIVE CONJUNCTIONS

Correlative conjunctions include *not only ... but also*, *either ... or*, *neither ... nor*, and *both ... and*. If a verb is placed before the first item in the correlative construction, then the verb need not be repeated. If the verb is placed after the first item in the correlative construction, then it must be placed after the second item as well.

Original   *She not only likes beach volleyball but also snow skiing.*

Correct   *She likes not only beach volleyball but also snow skiing.*

Correct   *She not only likes beach volleyball but also likes snow skiing.*

NOTE ❧ The first correct version above is arguably more popular.

Exercises

Rewrite the following sentences using parallel structure.
The suggested answers are on page 152.

1. Cannelloni has and always will be my favorite Italian dish.
2. Sheila is intrigued but not very proficient at handwriting analysis.
3. Massage creates a relaxing, therapeutic, and rejuvenating experience both for your body and your well-being.
4. Brian will not ask nor listen to any advice.
5. The cross-examination neither contributed nor detracted from the defendant's claim of innocence.
6. A good scientist not only thinks thoroughly but also creatively.
7. Either we forget our plans, or accept their proposal.
8. In addition to having more protein than meat does, the soybean has protein higher in quality than meat.
9. A dilemma facing many young professionals is whether to choose to work for money or to work for enjoyment.
10. Neither should one lie to another person nor be so blunt as to cause them embarrassment.

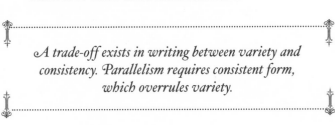

A trade-off exists in writing between variety and consistency. Parallelism requires consistent form, which overrules variety.

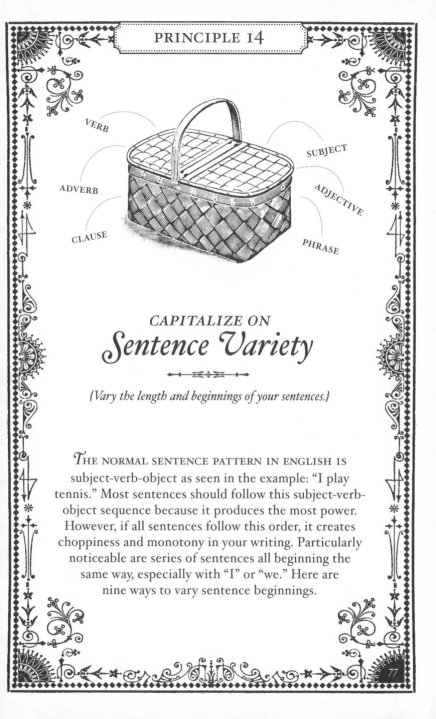

VERB

SUBJECT

ADVERB

ADJECTIVE

CLAUSE

PHRASE

CAPITALIZE ON
Sentence Variety

{Vary the length and beginnings of your sentences.}

THE NORMAL SENTENCE PATTERN IN ENGLISH IS subject-verb-object as seen in the example: "I play tennis." Most sentences should follow this subject-verb-object sequence because it produces the most power. However, if all sentences follow this order, it creates choppiness and monotony in your writing. Particularly noticeable are series of sentences all beginning the same way, especially with "I" or "we." Here are nine ways to vary sentence beginnings.

WITH A SUBJECT

> *Customers* can tell us why products sell if we take the time to listen to them.

WITH A PHRASE

> *For this reason*, no product is to be built until we know a market exists for it.

NOTE ☞ A phrase is a group of words that does not contain a verb.

WITH A CLAUSE

> *Because human beings are complex*, the sales process cannot be reduced to a simple formula.

NOTE ☞ A clause is a group of words that does contain a verb.

WITH A VERB

> *Try* not to eat and talk.

NOTE ☞ A verb is a word that expresses an action or a state of being.

WITH AN ADVERB

> *Understandably*, students like to hear entrepreneurs speak of rags-to-riches stories.

NOTE ☞ An adverb is a word that modifies a verb, an adjective, or another adverb.

WITH ADJECTIVES

> *Intelligent and compassionate*, Dorothy has the ingredients to be a leader.

NOTE ☞ An adjective is a word used to modify or describe a noun or pronoun.

WITH A GERUND

Allowing plenty of time, the law student started studying eight weeks before the bar exam.

NOTE ☞ A gerund is a noun formed with -*ing*. Informally it is said to be "a noun that looks like a verb."

WITH AN INFINITIVE

To be a monk, a person must be able to relinquish selfishness in order to concentrate on a higher goal.

NOTE ☞ An infinitive is a noun that is formed by a verb preceded by *to*.

WITH CORRELATIVE CONJUNCTIONS

Not only poverty but also pollution threatens the development of the third world.

If you must leave, then go now.

NOTE ☞ A conjunction is a word that joins or connects words, phrases, clauses, or sentences. A correlative conjunction joins parts of a sentence that are of equal weight. The four common correlative conjunctions include *not only ... but also*, *either ... or*, *neither ... nor*, and *both ... and*. Other correlative conjunctions include: *whether ... or*, *if ... then*, and *just as ... so too*.

For more on grammatical definitions and terms, please refer to the grammar section beginning on page 101.

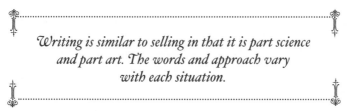

Writing is similar to selling in that it is part science and part art. The words and approach vary with each situation.

Exercises

For the purpose of practicing this principle, rearrange the following sentence to satisfy the different headings. You may have to change the content of the sentence for the purpose of this exercise. For suggested answers, see page 153.

> *Selling is difficult. It requires practical experience and personal initiative.*

1. With a Subject
2. With a Phrase
3. With a Clause
4. With a Verb
5. With an Adverb
6. With Adjectives
7. With a Gerund
8. With an Infinitive
9. With Correlative Conjunctions

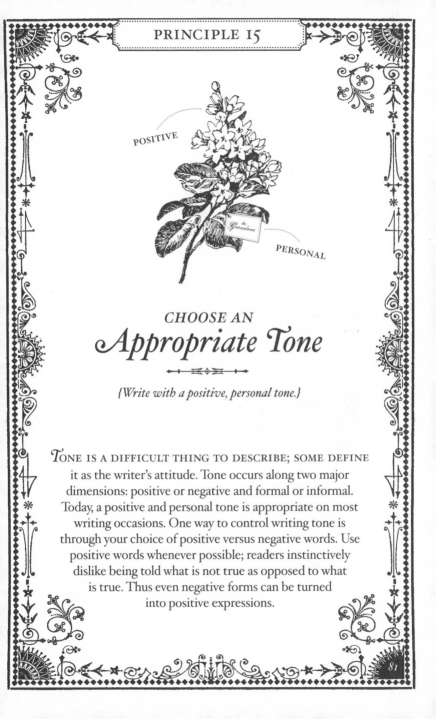

POSITIVE

PERSONAL

to Grandma

CHOOSE AN
Appropriate Tone

{Write with a positive, personal tone.}

TONE IS A DIFFICULT THING TO DESCRIBE; SOME DEFINE it as the writer's attitude. Tone occurs along two major dimensions: positive or negative and formal or informal. Today, a positive and personal tone is appropriate on most writing occasions. One way to control writing tone is through your choice of positive versus negative words. Use positive words whenever possible; readers instinctively dislike being told what is not true as opposed to what is true. Thus even negative forms can be turned into positive expressions.

POSITIVE VS. NEGATIVE TONE

Negative   *The store will close at 7 p.m.*

NOTE ☞ This uses a negative noun, "close."

Positive   *The store will remain open until 7 p.m.*

NOTE ☞ This uses a positive noun, "open."

Negative   *The plan is not sound.*

NOTE ☞ This uses a negative word; it tells us what isn't true as opposed to what is true.

Positive   *The plan has drawbacks.*

NOTE ☞ This states deficiencies in a positive manner; it tells us what is true.

FORMAL VS. INFORMAL TONE

Writing may have a formal or an informal tone. Two of the biggest factors in formality are the use of contractions and personal pronouns.

USE OF PERSONAL PRONOUNS

Add personal pronouns to make your writing more informal and personable.

No pronouns   *Please send any follow-up questions to the customer service department.*

Pronouns   *If you have any follow-up questions, please contact our customer service department.*

No pronouns   *The Chief Executive Officer is aware that strengthening product quality is the key to turning around the company.*

Pronouns   *As the Chief Executive Officer of our company, I view strengthening product quality as the key to a turnaround.*

A complete list of personal pronouns include:

1st person	I, me, my, mine, we, us, ours
2nd person	you, your, yours
3rd person	he, she, they, him, her, them, it, his, hers, its, their, theirs
Also	who, whom, whose

USE OF CONTRACTIONS

Add contractions (e.g., can't, isn't, shouldn't, won't) if you want your writing to come across as informal.

No contractions   *The stockholders have not voted on a new Chief Executive Officer.*

Contractions   *The stockholders haven't voted on a new Chief Executive Officer.*

Other factors also affect whether a document is considered formal, informal, or semi-formal (see next page). A personal letter or e-mail is typically informal while a business report is formal. A business letter is a good example of a semi-formal document: It usually contains informal characteristics (i.e., use of contractions, first-person pronouns, colloquial expressions, and simple or non-technical vocabulary) as well as formal characteristics (i.e., formal salutations and signatures).

> *NOTE* ☞ Although the practice of using contractions is now widespread, there are two theories on the effect of their use. The first theory or majority view is to use contractions because they reinforce a personal tone. The second or minority view is that although contractions are fine for use in writing e-mails and personal letters, it is preferable to avoid them in formal documents such as essays and reports.

FORMAL VS. INFORMAL TONE

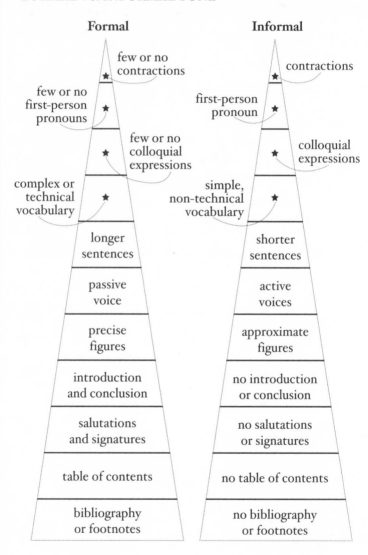

Formal

few or no contractions

few or no first-person pronouns

few or no colloquial expressions

complex or technical vocabulary

longer sentences

passive voice

precise figures

introduction and conclusion

salutations and signatures

table of contents

bibliography or footnotes

Informal

contractions

first-person pronoun

colloquial expressions

simple, non-technical vocabulary

shorter sentences

active voices

approximate figures

no introduction or conclusion

no salutations or signatures

no table of contents

no bibliography or footnotes

Exercise

Make this letter "warmer" by using a more positive and personal tone. This is a semi-formal document and it is recommended that contractions not be used. A suggested revision is on pages 153-154.

Dear Mr. Jones:

Comptronics Inc. deeply regrets the problems experienced with your notebook computer, Model 1580J. The company's engineers examined the unit and decided that the problems were so massive that they were not able to make repairs. The two remaining options are either to take a refund on the unit, or to request replacement with a new model. Please inform the service department of a decision, and Comptronics Inc. will quickly respond.

Sincerely,

Mr. Do Good
Service Representative
Comptronics Inc.

Tone is attitude. A formal tone is like formal attire that keeps distance between the writer and reader. Most writing favors an informal tone.

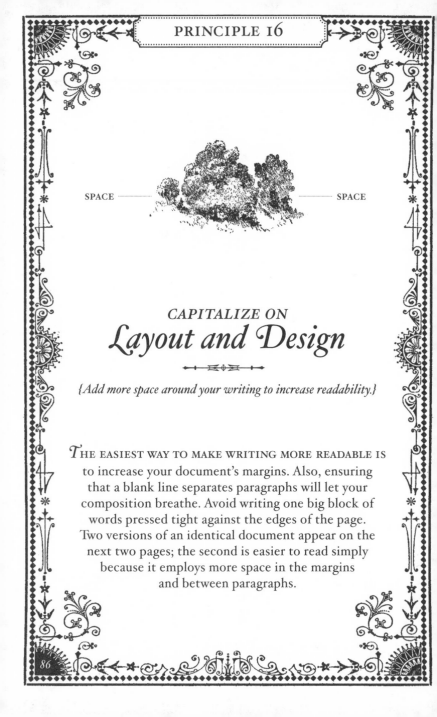

SPACE ⋯⋯⋯⋯⋯⋯⋯⋯⋯⋯⋯⋯⋯⋯⋯⋯⋯ SPACE

CAPITALIZE ON
Layout and Design

{Add more space around your writing to increase readability.}

THE EASIEST WAY TO MAKE WRITING MORE READABLE IS
to increase your document's margins. Also, ensuring
that a blank line separates paragraphs will let your
composition breathe. Avoid writing one big block of
words pressed tight against the edges of the page.
Two versions of an identical document appear on the
next two pages; the second is easier to read simply
because it employs more space in the margins
and between paragraphs.

ORIGINAL VERSION

You're in front of the computer screen. The page is still blank. Your thoughts are racing, your fingers are paralyzed. You're a smart person, so why the difficulty, the doubts. From the hall of darkness comes another thought—you're a failure. Your instinct is to fight. But the more you do, the more frustrated you get. You're a fish tangled in a net, going nowhere. Welcome to writer's block.

Forget about eliminating writer's block. Every writer experiences it on some level and on some occasions. The trick is to learn how to sidestep it when it suddenly arrives. Sneak around it. Dance around it. Just don't blame your muses for deserting you. Here are three important tips to use to combat writer's block.

1. Do a little research. Perhaps you don't know much about your topic and writer's block has set in. Go online and see what's out there. Ask some friends for their opinions or suggestions. The more you look into your topic, the more your topic will look into you. You'll invariably find some angle that will help you generate the interest or intrigue to start moving again.

2. Avoid procrastination. Try to do a little writing every day rather than leave your writing for one massive, all-out attack. The way a snake eats in one big gulp is hardly the way writers should write. Many people are great once they get started, but it's the getting started that's the hard part. Writing requires patience. It also often requires that you force yourself to write. Try writing an outline to break down your topic logically. Then make a schedule and stick to it.

3. Avoid perfectionism, close cousin of the fear of failure. If we don't write something striking, we fear our self image will be destroyed. Avoiding writing because we have set standards that are too high is unhealthy and unrealistic. Few darts hit the bulls-eye on the very first throw. Perhaps the best tip for overcoming perfectionism is to never write and edit at the same time. These are two separate processes. Get ideas down first. Straighten up things later.

IMPROVED VERSION

You're in front of the computer screen. The page is still blank. Your thoughts are racing, your fingers are paralyzed. You're a smart person, so why the difficulty, the doubts. From the hall of darkness comes another thought—you're a failure. Your instinct is to fight. But the more you do, the more frustrated you get. You're a fish tangled in a net, going nowhere. Welcome to writer's block.

Forget about eliminating writer's block. Every writer experiences it on some level and on some occasions. The trick is to learn how to sidestep it when it suddenly arrives. Sneak around it. Dance around it. Just don't blame your muses for deserting you. Here are three important tips to use to combat writer's block.

1. Do a little research. Perhaps you don't know much about your topic and writer's block has set in. Go online and see what's out there. Ask some friends for their opinions or suggestions. The more you look into your topic, the more your topic will look into you. You'll invariably find some angle that will help you generate the interest or intrigue to start moving again.

2. Avoid procrastination. Try to do a little writing every day rather than leave your writing for one massive, all out attack. The way a snake eats in one big gulp is hardly the way writers should write.

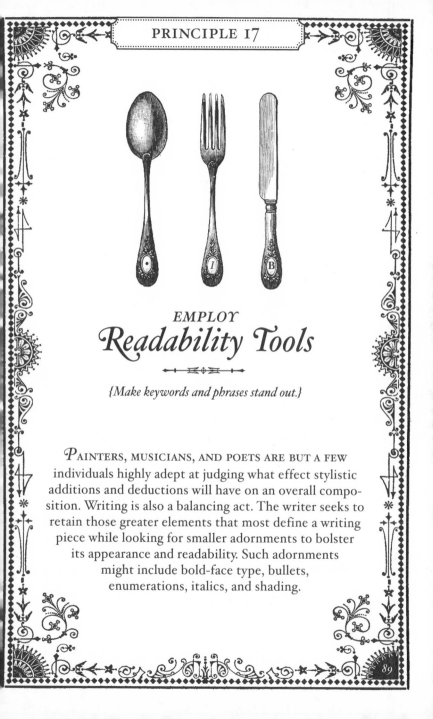

EMPLOY
Readability Tools

{Make keywords and phrases stand out.}

Painters, musicians, and poets are but a few individuals highly adept at judging what effect stylistic additions and deductions will have on an overall composition. Writing is also a balancing act. The writer seeks to retain those greater elements that most define a writing piece while looking for smaller adornments to bolster its appearance and readability. Such adornments might include bold-face type, bullets, enumerations, italics, and shading.

BOLD TYPE

Bolds may be used to emphasize keywords and help key ideas jump out at the reader. Bolds are especially useful for flyers, resumés, and other documents in which the reader may spend only a brief time reviewing. Underlining or capitalizing can do the same job as bold type, though care must be exercised not to overdo it. Full caps, if used extensively, can make a document difficult to read. One unwritten rule of editing is to never use bolds, full caps, and underlines together (ditto for bolds, italics, and underlines in combination). Be aware that if you use bold-face type too liberally, you will dull the effect and perhaps patronize the reader.

BULLETS

Bullets (•) are effective tools when paraphrasing information, especially when presenting information in short phrases when formal sentences are not required. Bullets are most commonly used when preparing resumés, slides, or flyers. Bullets are not, however, recommended for use in the main body of an essay or report.

ENUMERATIONS

Enumerations involve the numbering of points. Listing items by number is more formal but very useful for ordering ideas or data.

EXAMPLE

> *I feel that my greatest long-term contributions working in this field will be measured by (1) my ability to find ways to define and quantify, in dollars and cents, the benefits of ethics and corporate citizenship, and (2) my ability to sell corporations on the proactive benefits of these programs as a means to market the company, products, and employees.*

ITALICS

There is artistry in the occasional use of italics. Italics, like bolds, serve similar purposes. Think of using italics to highlight certain key words, especially those that show contrast, or for small words, especially negative words such as *not, no,* and *but*. Be careful of overusing italics because they are tiring on the eye and can make the page look busy.

SHADING

Shading creates contrast on the page, and can be a great device when formatting business reports. For example, you can highlight the start of each report section by using shaded section headings. Flyers also commonly use shading to call out information.

RESUMÉ EXAMPLE

The following is an excerpt from a resumé; resumés provide a classic example of the use of readability tools.

PROFESSIONAL EXPERIENCE

2003-present   **BANK OF AMERICA**, Hartford, Conn.
Financial Analyst
- Analyzed branch performance and devised new strategies to improve regional market share. Formulated a two-year marketing plan for two branches.
- Developed a new commission system and assisted in its implementation.
- Presented tax saving strategies and advice on investment portfolio compositions for principal clients.

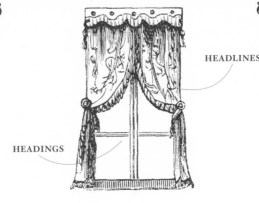

HEADLINES

HEADINGS

CONSIDER USING
Headings and Headlines

{Use headings and headlines to divide or summarize your writing.}

BECAUSE ORGANIZATION IS PARTICULARLY IMPORTANT in academic writing, which tends to be longer, and because time and money are of critical importance in business, both headings and headlines help convey information efficiently. Headlines are similar to headings; the difference lies in their length and purpose. Headings are usually a couple of words in length; headlines are usually a line or two in length. The purpose of headings is to divide information under sections; the primary purpose of headlines is to summarize or paraphrase information that follows.

With the use of headings in the document below, the compiler is able to direct the reader's attention; without headings, the reader would have a harder job of accessing the information efficiently.

EFFECTIVE USE OF HEADINGS

Color
The most desirable diamonds are colorless. The color scale starts at D and descends through Z. Although the best color is D (colorless), diamonds also come in a range of natural fancy tones, such as blue, pink, green, and red. Believe it or not, these fancy diamonds are particularly rare, and like their colorless counterparts, can also fetch a high price tag.

Clarity
Gemologists refer to imperfections in diamond clarity as "inclusions"; the fewer inclusions, the more valuable the stone.

Cut
What makes a diamond stand out beyond any other precious gemstone? Certainly the way it sparkles. While nature determines the color and clarity of a stone, diamond cut is solely dependent upon the skill of the cutter.

Carat Weight
The word carat comes from the carob seeds that were used to balance scales in ancient times. Carat therefore refers to size. It is not necessarily true that the larger the carat, the more valuable the diamond. The value of a stone will always be a combination of the four Cs: color, clarity, cut, and carat size.

Headlines are effective tools in summarizing complete sections of a business report or personal essay.

EFFECTIVE USE OF HEADLINES

The Land, Sea, and Sky Must Guide Me

The land, the sky, and the sea: These three environments and the experiences they have given me have influenced and helped shape who I am today.

When I go back to the land in the northern part of Denmark, I walk across the fields and hear the birds singing. The land has taught me to appreciate my base and family stability. _____ _____ _____ .

The smallest corals in bright colors can be poisonous while the sharks may be friendly. When scuba diving, I have learned to expect the unexpected. _____ _____ _____ _____ .

The sky is a reminder that many things are possible even though they seem beyond our reach. Sky diving has encouraged me to stretch and reach new heights. _____ _____ _____ .

One of the big challenges I am meeting in life is the challenge of being successful in both my personal and career life. In meeting these challenges, all of my influences must guide me—the land, the sea, and the sky.

KEEP YOUR WRITING
Gender Neutral

{Avoid using the masculine generic to refer to both genders.}

THE MASCULINE GENERIC REFERS TO THE SOLE USE OF the pronoun "he" or "him" when referring to situations involving both genders. Avoid using "he" when referring to either a he or a she; likewise, avoid using "him" when referring to either a him or a her. Be sensitive in acknowledging both sexes. Because 50 percent of any general readership is likely female, it is not only politically astute but fair-minded to avoid using the masculine generic.

Consider the following sentences from a female perspective.

ORIGINAL

> *Today's chief executive must be extremely well rounded. He must not only be corporate and civic minded but also be internationally focused and entrepreneurially spirited.*

There are essentially two ways to remedy this. Replace "he" with "he or she," or recast the sentence in the plural, using "they" or "them."

BETTER

> *Today's chief executive must be extremely well rounded. He or she must not only be corporate and civic minded but also be internationally focused and entrepreneurially spirited.*

EQUALLY PROPER

> *Today's chief executives must be extremely well rounded. They must not only be corporate and civic minded but also be internationally focused and entrepreneurially spirited.*

A final way to address the problem, especially when writing longer documents, is to alternate between the use of "he" and "she." The disadvantage in this approach, however, is that the arbitrary, alternate use of these two pronouns may annoy the reader.

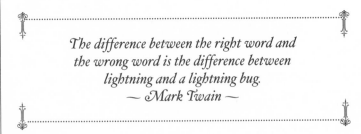

> *The difference between the right word and the wrong word is the difference between lightning and a lightning bug.*
> *— Mark Twain —*

We must also watch for and replace words that represent the masculine generic. Here is a partial list:

Masculine Generic	Better
ad man	advertising executive
anchorman	anchor
chairman	chair, chairperson
Englishmen	the English
fireman	firefighter
man-hours	work-hours, person-hours
mankind	humans, humankind, humanity
policeman	police officer
postman, mailman	mail carrier, postal agent
salesman	salesperson, sales representative
self-made man	self-made person
businessman	businessperson
congressman	member of Congress, Congressional Representative
spokesman	spokesperson
landlord	land owner
layman	layperson
manmade	synthetic, artificial
workman	worker

It is sometimes necessary to replace the feminine generic:

Feminine Generic	Better
housewife	homemaker
maiden name	birth name, former name
stewardess	flight attendant
cleaning lady/maid	domestic, housekeeper
secretary (office)	office assistant

GO BACK AND
Rework Your Writing

{Wait until your writing stands still before you call it finished.}

RARE IS THE WRITER WHO CAN SIT DOWN AND KNOCK out a perfect writing draft without corrections. Most proficient writers take at least three drafts to finish short writing works. For example, you may be writing a cover letter to accompany your updated resume. First, you write to get your ideas down on paper. Second, you edit through what you have written, add detail, make connections, and make corrections. Third, you wait twenty-four hours and reread, making minor changes. The longer the work, the more times this process is repeated for individual sections.

The number of drafts required for an entire work depends on the length of the work and its complexity. A two-line office memo is likely to be done in a single draft because it is short and simple. A one-page poem might take more than a dozen drafts because it is longer and more difficult.

WHEN IS IT REALLY FINISHED?

Making changes to your writing is annoying and grueling. But eventually, with changes made, you will likely be satisfied with what you have written and not want to add or delete anything. This is the point at which your writing is finished—your writing is "standing still." Unpolished writing is like shifting sand in a desert storm. Eventually the storm ceases, and the sand sits still.

The word "finished," when referring to writing, should really be enclosed in quotation marks because writing is never actually finished. With respect to writing done for everyday purposes, completion is an end in itself. However, for more permanent writing works, such as novels, writing can be continued because it can always be improved. Even published books can be reworked and reedited. Weeks, months, and years after a book is published, an author will inevitably contemplate changes.

APPRECIATE THE PROCESS

Writing is a creative process. You discover things as you force yourself to write. What is especially satisfying is turning junk writing into something worthwhile. When you put together a lengthy piece, such as a personal essay or business report, you will naturally begin by writing some areas well. Other areas you will not be satisfied with, and those must be reworked.

Most people hate reworking their writing. It is human nature. The pressure and agony of writing is one reason why alcohol has been humorously dubbed "the occupational hazard of professional writers." It is not writing per se, but the rewriting and redrafting process that can drive a person to drink. Worse is the reality of knowing that even before you begin to write—no matter how well you write—your writing will require revision. Fortunately, for most students and business professionals, the everyday writing process is not filled with the same emotional highs and lows as it is for a person making a living from writing.

It is a great feeling to look at something you wrote a long time ago, be it an old college essay, business report, personal letter, or poem, and say to yourself, "Wow this is funny. Some of it blows me away! How did I come up with it?" There is no absolute answer. Skill, luck, boldness, and naiveté are key ingredients in the writing process.

> *The pleasure of the first draft lies in deceiving yourself that it is quite close to the real thing. The pleasure of the subsequent drafts lies partly in realizing that you haven't been gulled by the first draft.*
> *— Julian Barnes —*

RULES:
- ALWAYS CHECK THE SIZE OF GRANDMA'S TEETH
- NOTICE IF GRANDMA HAS GROWN EARS
- IF GRANDMA HAS DEVELOPED FUR... RUN!

30 RULES *of Grammar*

{Learn the basics of grammar and the eight parts of speech.}

IN THIS SECTION WE TALK OF GRAMMAR RULES AS opposed to writing principles. Grammar differs from structure, style, and readability in that only grammar can be described as correct or incorrect, right or wrong. Structure, style, and readability can be effective or less effective, better or worse. For example, the active voice is superior to the passive voice, but it is not correct to say that the use of the passive voice is wrong. Failure to provide proper space around a document is not a clear violation of writing technique. And there is no magic line that separates succinct writing from verbosity.

The ensuing discussion covers the major topical areas of grammar, grouped according to the eight parts of speech. This coverage is not meant to be exhaustive, but rather to focus on common problem areas. Readers who want a more technical, in-depth analysis should consult a handbook of English grammar and usage.

THE EIGHT PARTS OF SPEECH

The eight parts of speech in the English language are:

1. Nouns
2. Pronouns
3. Adjectives
4. Verbs
5. Adverbs
6. Prepositions
7. Conjunctions
8. Interjections

Any given part of speech may have one or more of the following characteristics: (1) gender (2) number (3) person (4) case (5) voice (6) mood, and (7) tense. In summary, gender is either masculine or feminine; number is either singular or plural; person may be first person, second person, or third person; case may be subjective, objective, or possessive; voice is either active or passive; mood may be indicative, imperative, or subjunctive; and tense is either simple or progressive. These characteristics are introduced here to briefly familiarize the reader with them and to help the reader recognize them when or if doing more in-depth research at a later point.

> *NOTE* ⌘ Adjectives, adverbs, conjunctions, and interjections do not
> have gender, number, person, case, voice, mood, or tense. The matching
> of a given part of speech with each of the above characteristics is the
> primary "cause" of grammar.

NOUNS

Overview Other than uncertainty as to when to capitalize a word or form the possessive, there are few problem areas relating to the use of nouns.

Definition A noun is a word that names a person, place, or thing.

Example: Sally is a nice person and you can speak freely with her.

Major classification of nouns Proper nouns (specific names)
Examples: Mrs. Jones, Boston, Budweiser

Common nouns (general classes)
Examples: man, trout, umbrella

Concrete nouns (tangibles)
Examples: tree, car, pencil

Abstract nouns (ideas, qualities)
Examples: honor, jealousy

Singular nouns (individuals)
Examples: person, dog, flower

Collective nouns (group)
Examples: crowd, flock, jury

PRONOUNS

Overview — Several problem areas relate to the use of pronouns; most center on ambiguous pronoun reference.

Definition — A pronoun is a word used in place of a noun or another pronoun.

Example: Sally is a nice person and <u>you</u> can speak freely with <u>her</u>.

Major classification of pronouns — Personal pronouns
Examples: I, you, he/she, it, we, they

Relative pronouns
Examples: who, which, what, that

Interrogative pronouns
Examples: who, which, what

Demonstrative pronouns
These include: this, that, these, those

Indefinite pronouns
Examples: all, anybody, each, either

Reflexive pronouns
Examples: himself, herself, ourselves, themselves

Grammar — Pronouns have gender, number, person and case, but not voice, mood, or tense.

Rule 1: Who vs. Whom

If *he*, *she*, or *they* can be substituted for the pronoun in context, the correct form is *who*. If *him*, *her*, or *them* can be substituted, the correct form is *whom*.

Rule 2: Indefinite Pronouns

Indefinite pronouns such as *everybody, everyone, anyone,* and *anything* are always singular.

Certain indefinite pronouns are <u>always singular</u>. These include *anybody, anyone, anything, everybody, everyone, every one, somebody, someone, some one, either, neither, no one, one, each.*

Certain indefinite pronouns are <u>always plural</u>. These include *both, few, many, several.*

Still other indefinite pronouns can be <u>either singular or plural</u>. These include *some, all, any, most, none.*

> **Correct**   *Some of the speech was heartwarming.*

> **Correct**   *Some of the comedians were hilarious.*

Rule 3: Pronouns in the Objective Form

Pronouns take their objective form when they are the direct objects of prepositions.

> **Incorrect** *The present is from Beth and she.*

> **Correct**   *The present is from Beth and her.*

Rule 4: Pronouns in the Subjective Form

Pronouns take their subjective form when used in direct comparisons.

Incorrect *We are better swimmers than them.*

Correct *We are better swimmers than they.*

Rule 5: Reflexive Pronouns

Do not use a reflexive pronoun if an ordinary personal pronoun will suffice. Reflexive pronouns include *myself*, *himself*, *yourself*, *themselves*.

[number 3]
ADJECTIVES

Overview Problems with adjectives center on distinguishing adjectives from adverbs and using the comparative versus superlative forms of comparison.

Definition An adjective is a word used to modify or describe a noun or pronoun.

Example: Sally is a <u>nice</u> person and you can speak freely with her.

Grammar Adjectives do not have gender, number, person, case, voice, mood, or tense.

Rule 6: Comparatives and Superlatives

The superlative is used when comparing three or more persons or things; the comparative is used when comparing exactly two persons or things.

Take the words *wealthier* and *wealthiest*: *Wealthier* is an example of the comparative, and *wealthiest* is an example of a superlative.

PERSONAL PRONOUNS

The table below presents personal pronouns in all genders, numbers, persons, and cases.

Personal Pronouns	Subjective	Possessive	Objective
1st-person singular	I	my, mine	me
2nd-person singular	you	your, yours	you
3rd-person singular	he, she, it	his, hers, its	him, her, it
1st-person plural	we	our, ours	us
2nd-person plural	you	your, yours	you
3rd-person plural	they	their, theirs	them
who	who	whose	whom

Example   *Todd is wealthier than Jim. In fact, Todd is the wealthiest of his friends.*

Rule 7: Singular and Plural Verbs

Singular subjects take singular verbs; plural or compound subjects take plural verbs.

Rule 8: Correlative Conjunction Agreement

To determine whether a verb that follows an *either ... or* or *neither ... nor* construction is singular or plural, match the verb with the word which immediately follows the word *or* or *nor*.

Rule 9: Subjunctive Mood

The subjunctive mood uses the verb *were* instead of *was* and expresses a hypothetical possibility, wish, desire, or situation that is opposite actual fact.

In written and especially spoken English, the subjunctive is less frequently used. The writer or speaker may choose to err on the side of formality and tradition.

Examples   *I wish she was here now.*
(contemporary but informal)

I wish she were here now.
(traditional and formal)

If situations are not contrary to fact or the writer is unsure whether the situation is contrary to fact, then the subjunctive is not used.

> *Example*   *If it <u>was</u> raining in London today, my parents*
>   *would not have gone on a tour of the Botanical*
>   *Gardens.*

If we do not know whether it was actually raining in London, use *was*. If we know for a fact that it is not raining in London, use *were*.

> *Example*   *If I <u>was</u> a guitar player, wouldn't I play my*
>   *best songs at a concert?*

Assuming that you are a guitar player, use *was*. If you are not a guitar player, then use *were*.

Rule 10: Consistent Verb Tenses

Use consistent verb tenses. Generally speaking, we must keep tenses in the past, present, or future. The simple past tense is used for events that happened at definite points in the past. The past perfect tense is used to show a sequence between two past tense events; the first of the two past events is preceded by *had*.

The present perfect tense (e.g., *has* or *have*) indicates that an action that started in the past also continues into the present.

The future tense signals events which have not yet happened, while the future perfect tense shows a sequence between two future events.

Verb Charts A and B on pages 112–113 illustrate this more clearly.

Overview	Problems with verbs center largely on subject-verb agreement and on distinguishing the past-perfect verb tense from the present-perfect verb tense.
Definition	A verb is a word that expresses an action or a state of being.
	Example: Sally is a nice person and you <u>can speak</u> freely with her.
Major classification of verbs	Principal verbs *Example: spoken*
	Auxiliary verbs *Example: have spoken*
	Transitive verbs (requires object) *Example: They posted a card on her door.*
	Intransitive verbs (doesn't require object) *Example: He waits.*
	Regular verbs (participle formed with *-ed*) *Example: travel, traveled, have traveled*
	Irregular verbs (not formed with *-ed*) *Example: go, went, have gone*
Grammar	Verbs have voice, mood, tense, number, and person but not gender or case.

VERBALS

Verbals, which include participles, gerunds, and infinitives, are not one of the eight parts of speech, but they are words and phrases that function as nouns, adjectives, and other parts of speech.

Participles   Usually end in *-ing* or *-ed* and function as adjectives.

   Examples: Cars parked in no parking zones will be towed. Let sleeping dogs lie.

Gerunds   End in *-ing* and function as nouns. They may also be the subject of a sentence.

   Examples: Studying languages is rewarding. Eating vegetables is good for you.

   NOTE ☞ "Eating vegetables" and "studying languages" are both gerund phrases that act as the singular subjects of each sentence.

Infinitives   Combine the basic form of a verb with *to*. Infinitives may function as nouns, adjectives, or adverbs. When used as a noun, they may also serve as the subject of a sentence.

   Examples: Visitors come to see famous sites. To err is human.

Rule 11: Verbal Phrases

Gerunds and infinitives are always singular and take singular verbs.

VERB CHART A
THE SIMPLE AND PROGRESSIVE VERB FORMS

	Simple Form	Progressive Form
Present	I travel	I am traveling
Past	I traveled	I was traveling
Future	I will travel	I will be traveling
Present Perfect	I have traveled	I have been traveling
Past Perfect	I had traveled	I had been traveling
Future Perfect	I will have traveled	I will have been traveling

VERB CHART B
VISUALIZING THE SIX VERB TENSES

Tense	Example	Summary
Simple Present	I study physics.	Expresses events or situations that currently exist including the near past and near present.
Simple Past	I studied physics.	Expresses events or situations that existed in the past.
Simple Future	I will study physics.	Expresses events or situations that will exist in the future.
Present Perfect	I have studied physics.	Expresses events or situations that existed in the past but that touch the present.
Past Perfect	I had studied physics in high school before I went to college.	Expresses events or situations in the past, one of which occurred before the other.
Future Perfect	By the time I graduate from college, I will have studied for four years.	Expresses events or situations in the future, one of which will occur after the other.

ADVERBS

Overview   Other than distinguishing adverbs from adjectives, there are few problem areas relating to adverbs.

Definition   An adverb is a word that modifies a verb, an adjective, or another adverb.

Example: Sally is a nice person and you can speak <u>freely</u> with her.

Grammar   Adverbs do not have gender, number, person, case, voice, mood, or tense.

PREPOSITIONS

Overview   There are few problem areas relating to the use of prepositions. However, as prepositions are used to form many idiomatic expressions, they can be confusing for students learning English as a foreign language.

Definition   A preposition is a word that shows a relationship between two or more words.

Example: Sally is a nice person and you can speak freely <u>with</u> her.

Grammar   Prepositions do not have gender, number, person, case, voice, mood, or tense.

CONJUNCTIONS

Overview With respect to conjunctions, potential problems arise when using correlative conjunctions and trying to maintain parallelism.

Definition A conjunction is a word that joins or connects words, phrases, clauses, or sentences.

Example: Sally is a nice person <u>and</u> you can speak freely with her.

Major classification of conjunctions Coordinating Conjunctions
Examples: and, but, or, nor, for, so, yet

Subordinating Conjunctions
Examples: although, because, before, if, since, unless, when, where

Correlative Conjunctions
Examples: both … and, either … or, neither … nor, not only … but (also), whether … or

Grammar Conjunctions do not have gender, number, person, case, voice, mood, or tense.

⊱ INTERJECTIONS ⊰

Overview   There are few problems relating to the use of interjections.

Definition   An interjection is a word or a term that denotes a strong or sudden feeling.

                Example: Sally is a nice person and you can speak freely with her. <u>Wow!</u>

Grammar   Interjections do not have gender, number, person, case, voice, mood, or tense.

Exercises

The number of each quiz item refers back to the rule that will help you determine the correct answer. The solution is on pages 154-158.

1a. The woman (who / whom) is responsible for city planning is Mrs. Green.

1b. This gift is intended for (who / whom)?

2a. Everybody should mind (his or her / their) own business.

2b. Few of the students (is / are) ready for the test.

2c. None of the candidates (has / have) any previous political experience.

2d. None of the story (makes / make) sense.

3a. Between you and (I / me), this plan makes a lot of sense.

3b. People like you and (I / me) should know better.

3c. Will you come and speak to Cecelia and (I / me)?

3d. Do not ask for (who / whom) the bell tolls.

3e. Come celebrate the New Year with Christina and (I / me).

4a. He is taller than (I / me).

4b My sister sings better than (she / her).

5a. Young Robert hurt (him / himself) while climbing alone.

5b. The teacher told Julie and (me / myself) to stop talking.

6a. Between Tom and Brenda, Tom is the (better / best) student.

6b. Among all the students, Jeff is the (better / best) in math.

7a. The president and key members of his cabinet (was / were) present at the meeting.

7b. The purpose of the executive, administrative, and legislative branches of government (is / are) to provide a system of checks and balances.

8a. Either Yohan or Cecilia (is / are) qualified to act as manager.

8b. Neither Julie nor her sisters (is / are) going on vacation.

9a. If I (was / were) you, I would be feeling optimistic.

9b. Sometimes she wishes she (was / were) on a tropical island, enjoying drinks at sunset.

10a. My dog (barks / barked) as soon as he sees our neighbor's cat.

10b. Yesterday afternoon, without warning, smoked (filled / had filled) the sky and sirens sounded.

10c. Tomorrow, I will (go / have gone) to the party.

10d. Larry (studied / had studied) Russian for five years before he went to work in Moscow.

10e. A recent study has found that many workers (have / had) opted for lower pay in exchange for more days off.

10f. By the time I call her, she (left / will have left) the office.

11a. Implementing the consultants' recommendations (is / are) difficult.

11b. Entertaining multiple goals (makes / make) a person's life stressful.

[additional]

GRAMMAR RULES

The following rules apply to diction or word choice. The words you choose affect how clear, correct, and effective your writing is.

Rule 12: Possessives and Contractions

Distinguish between possessives and contractions. These are probably the most frequent errors you will find in daily e-mails and memos.

There is an adverb; *their* is a possessive pronoun; *they're* is a contraction for *they are*.

> *Examples*   *There is* nothing to worry about.
>
> *Their* car is the most expensive I have ever ridden in.
>
> *They're* a strange couple.

Its is a possessive pronoun; *it's* is a contraction for *it is*.

> *Examples*   *The world has lost <u>its</u> meaning*
>
> *<u>It's</u> time to quit.*

Your is a possessive pronoun; *you're* is a contraction for *you are*.

> *Examples*   *This is <u>your</u> book.*
>
> *<u>You're</u> becoming the person you want to be.*

Whose is a possessive pronoun; *who's* is a contraction for *who is*.

> *Examples*   *<u>Whose</u> umbrella did I find?*
>
> *He is the one <u>who's</u> most likely to be voted valedictorian.*

Lets is a verb meaning "to allow or permit"; *let's* is a contraction for "let us."

> *Examples*   *Technology <u>lets us</u> live more easily.*
>
> *<u>Let's</u> not forget those who fought for our freedom.*

Rule 13: Than vs. Then

Distinguish between *than* and *then*. *Than* is a conjunction used in making comparisons. *Then* is an adverb indicating time.

> *Examples*   *There is a controversy over whether the Petronas Towers in Malaysia are taller <u>than</u> the Sears Tower in Chicago.*
>
> *Finish your work first, <u>then</u> give me a call.*

Rule 14: All Together vs. Altogether

All together means in one group. *Altogether* means completely or entirely.

> Examples We were *all together* for the holidays.
>
> That piece of advice sounds *altogether* wrong.

Rule 15: All Ready vs. Already

All ready means entirely ready or prepared. *Already* means before or previously, but may also mean now or so soon.

> Examples Contingency plans ensure that military personnel are *all ready* in case of an attack. (entirely ready or prepared)
>
> I have *already* tried the newest brand. (before or previously)
>
> Is it dinnertime *already*? (now or so soon)

Rule 16: Maybe vs. May Be

Maybe is an adverb meaning perhaps. *May be* is a verb phrase.

> Examples *Maybe* it is time to call it quits.
>
> It *may be* necessary to resort to extreme measures.

Rule 17: Between vs. Among

Use *between* to discuss two things. Use *among* to discuss three or more things.

Examples   *The jackpot was divided <u>between</u> two winners.*

The jackpot was divided <u>among</u> five winners.

Rule 18: Each Other vs. One Another

Use *each other* when referring to two people. Use *one another* when referring to more than two people.

Examples   *The two athletes helped <u>each other</u>.*

Olympic athletes compete against <u>one another</u>.

Rule 19: Fewer vs. Less

Fewer refers to things that can be counted, such as people or things. *Less* refers to things that cannot be counted, such as water or sand.

Examples   *<u>Fewer</u> students remained in class after the midterm exam.*

There is <u>less</u> milk in my glass.

Rule 20: Number vs. Amount

Use *number* to refer to things that can be counted. Use *amount* to refer to things that cannot be counted.

Examples   *The <u>number</u> of marbles in the bag is seven.*

The <u>amount</u> of water in the stream has dwindled considerably.

Rule 21: Affect vs. Effect

Affect is a verb meaning to influence; *effect* is a noun meaning result; *effect* is also a verb meaning to bring about.

Examples   *The change in policy will not <u>affect</u> our pay.*

                           He wants to <u>effect</u> a change in the schedule.

                           The long-term <u>effect</u> of global warming is unclear.

Rule 22: That vs. Which

That is used for restrictive clauses; *which* is used for nonrestrictive clauses. Restrictive phrases are essential to meaning, whereas nonrestrictive phrases are not. Nonrestrictive phrases are enclosed by commas; restrictive phrases are not.

Examples   *The book <u>that</u> is red is the one you need for English class.*

                           The blue book, <u>which</u> is on the top shelf, is authored by our professor.

Rule 23: Farther vs. Further

Use *farther* when referring to distance. Use *further* in all other cases, particularly when referring to extent or degree.

Examples   *The town is one mile <u>farther</u> along the road.*

                           We must pursue this idea <u>further</u>.

Rule 24: If vs. Whether

Use *if* to express one possibility. Use *whether* to express two or more possibilities.

Examples   *Success depends on <u>whether</u> one has desire and determination.*

The company claims that you will be successful if you listen to their tapes on motivation.

Rule 25: Compare To vs. Compare With

Use *compare to* in pointing out similarities. Use *compare with* in pointing out differences.

> Examples   *He compared Kennedy to Lincoln.*
> (He pointed out similarities.)
>
> *He compared Kennedy with Nixon.*
> (He pointed out differences.)

Rule 26: Differ From vs. Differ With

Use *differ from* in discussing characteristics. Use *differ with* to convey the idea of disagreement.

> Examples   *American English differs from British English.*
>
> *The clerk differs with her manager on his decision to hire an additional sales person.*

Rule 27: Infer vs. Imply

Infer means to draw a conclusion; readers or listeners infer. *Imply* means to hint or suggest; speakers or writers imply.

> Examples   *I infer from your letter that travel conditions have improved.*
>
> *Do you mean to imply that travel conditions have improved?*

Rule 28: Passed vs. Past

Passed functions as a verb; *past* functions as a noun, adjective, or preposition.

> *Examples* Yesterday, Cindy found out that she <u>passed</u> her three-hour medical exam.
>
> The proactive mind does not dwell on events of the <u>past</u>.

Rule 29: Like vs. As

One way to distinguish between *like* and *as* is that *like* is used in phrases whereas *as* is used in clauses.

> *She sings <u>like</u> an angel.*
>
> **NOTE** ☞ "Like an angel" is a phrase. A phrase is a group of words that does not contain a verb.

> *She sings <u>as</u> an angel sings.*
>
> **NOTE** ☞ "As an angel sings" is a clause. A clause is a group of words that does contain a verb.

> *No one plays golf <u>as</u> Tiger Woods does.*
>
> **NOTE** ☞ "As Tiger Woods does" is a clause, so the use of *like* is not correct.

> *<u>Like</u> many other top professional athletes, Tiger Woods makes more money from endorsements than from competition.*
>
> **NOTE** ☞ "Like many other top professional athletes" is a phrase, so the use of *as* would be incorrect.

Such as is used for listing items in a series. Frequently the word *like* is incorrectly substituted for *such as*.

> *Example*   *A beginning rugby player must master many different skills <u>such as</u> running and passing, blocking and tackling, and scrum control.*

Rule 30: Lie vs. Lay

In the present tense, *lie* means to rest and *lay* means to put or to place.

Lie is an intransitive verb (a verb that does not require a direct object to complete its meaning), while *lay* is a transitive verb (a verb that requires a direct object to complete its meaning).

LIE (TO REST OR TO RECLINE)

Present	*Lie on the sofa.*
Past	*He lay down for an hour.*
Perfect Participle	*He has lain there for an hour.*
Present Participle	*It was nearly noon and he was still lying on the sofa.*

LAY (TO PUT OR TO PLACE)

Present	*Lay the book on the table.*
Past	*He laid the book there yesterday.*
Perfect Participle	*He has laid the book there many times.*
Present Participle	*Laying the book on the table, she stood up and left the room.*

STANDARD VS. NONSTANDARD PHRASES

Here are common misusages to watch for.

Standard	Nonstandard
A lot	Alot
Considered to be	Considered as
In comparison to	In comparison with
In contrast to	In contrast with
Regarded as	Regarded to be
Regardless	Irregardless
Would have	Would of
With regard to	With regards to
Could have	Could of
Might have	Might of
In regard to	In regards to
Should have	Should of
Depicted as	Depicted to be

NOTE ☞ Certain words and phrases may be used interchangeably. Some common examples include *rather than* vs. *instead of*, and *different from* vs. *different than*, *toward* vs. *towards*, *anyone* vs. *any one*, *everyone* vs. *every one*, and *cannot* vs. *can not*. It is important to note that language changes over time and there is not 100 percent agreement as to what grammatical forms are considered incorrect and what words or phrases are considered non-standard. From one grammar handbook to another and from one dictionary to another, slight differences may arise. Interestingly, lexicographers struggle between the opposing forces of prescribing and describing language. Should they prescribe or dictate what the correct forms of language are or should they simply describe and record language as it is used by a majority of persons?

BEAT AROUND
THE BUSH

USING CORRECT
Grammatical Idioms

{Know the right way to express idiomatic phrases.}

IDIOMS, LIKE GRAMMAR, ARE CORRECT OR INCORRECT.
They are expressions that have gained acceptance
through the passing of time and usually have non-literal
meanings, such as "You're pulling my leg." Grammatical
idioms, as included here, do not have non-literal
meanings, and they usually involve the correct
use of a preposition. Here are one dozen
recurring grammatical idioms.

BETWEEN X AND Y

Correct *A choice must be made <u>between</u> blue <u>and</u> green.*

Incorrect *A choice must be made <u>between</u> blue <u>or</u> green.*

CREDIT X WITH HAVING

Correct *Many <u>credit</u> Gutenberg <u>with having</u> invented the movable-type press.*

Incorrect *Many <u>credit</u> Gutenberg <u>as having</u> invented the movable-type press.*

DISTINGUISHING X FROM Y

Correct *Only experts can <u>distinguish</u> a masterpiece <u>from</u> a fake.*

Incorrect *Only experts can <u>distinguish</u> a masterpiece <u>and</u> a fake.*

DO SO

Correct *Although doctors have the technology to perform brain transplants, there is no clear evidence that they can <u>do so</u>.*

Incorrect *Although doctors have the technology to perform brain transplants, there is no clear evidence that they can <u>do it</u>.*

FROM X RATHER THAN FROM Y

Correct *The majority of discoveries result <u>from</u> meticulous research <u>rather than</u> from sudden inspiration.*

Incorrect *The majority of discoveries result <u>from</u> meticulous research <u>instead of</u> sudden inspiration.*

FROM X TO Y

Correct *The population of Africa has grown from 530 million in 1960 to 700 million in 1990.*

Incorrect *The population of Africa has grown from 530 million in 1960 up to 700 million in 1990.*

MORE ... THAN / LESS ... THAN

Correct *There are more students today applying to graduate school than there were ten years ago.*

Incorrect *There are more / less students today applying to graduate school compared with ten years ago.*

Incorrect *There are more / less students today applying to graduate school compared to ten years ago.*

PREFER TO

Correct *I prefer fish to chicken.*

Incorrect *I prefer fish over chicken.*

RECOVER FROM

Correct *Someday, it may be worthwhile to try to recover salt from saltwater.*

Incorrect *Someday, it may be worthwhile to try to recover salt out of saltwater.*

TYING X TO Y

Correct *The author does a good job of tying motivational theory to obtainable results.*

Incorrect *The author does a good job of tying motivational theory with obtainable results.*

IN COMPARISON TO

Correct   *In comparison to France, Luxembourg is an amazingly small country.*

Incorrect   *In comparison with France, Luxembourg is an amazingly small country.*

IN CONTRAST TO

Correct   *Pete Sampras won Wimbledon with a classic tennis style in contrast to Bjorn Borg, who captured his titles using an unorthodox playing style.*

Incorrect   *Pete Sampras won Wimbledon with a classic tennis style in contrast with Bjorn Borg, who captured his titles using an unorthodox playing style.*

COLON

SEMI-COLON

A FEW HIGHLIGHTS ON
Correct Punctuation

+—◄◼◆◼►—+

{Know the basics of commas and semicolons.}

IN SPOKEN ENGLISH, WE CAN CONVEY OUR MEANING with the assistance of voice and body language: waving hands, rolling eyes, raising eyebrows, stress, rhythm, intonations, pauses, and even repeated sentences. In written language, we do not have such an arsenal of props: This is the unenviable job of punctuation. Mastery of punctuation, along with spelling and capitalization, requires in-depth review, and is not the focus of this book. But two key areas—commas and semi-colons—are addressed because they represent some of the most common punctuation errors.

COMMAS

It is said that 90 percent of writers can use the comma correctly 75 percent of the time, but only 1 percent of writers can use the comma correctly 99 percent of the time. The comma is often used and often used incorrectly. The well-known advice that advocates the use of the comma whenever you pause is terribly misleading. Arguably the best way to master the comma is to think of the comma as categorized into one of four types: listing comma, joining comma, bracketing comma, or omission comma.

LISTING COMMA

A listing comma separates items in a series. If more than two items are listed in a series, they should be separated by commas. The final comma in the series, the one that precedes the word *and*, is optional.

> **Correct** *A tostada is a tortilla fried until crisp, usually topped with a variety of ingredients such as shredded meat or chicken, refried beans, lettuce, tomatoes, and cheese.*

> **Correct** *A tostada is a tortilla fried until crisp, usually topped with a variety of ingredients such as shredded meat or chicken, refried beans, lettuce, tomatoes and cheese.*

Do not place commas before the first element of a series or after the last element.

> **Incorrect** *The classic investment portfolio consists of, stocks, bonds, and short-term deposits*

> **Incorrect** *Conversation, champagne, and party favors, were the highlights of our office party.*

BRACKETING COMMA

Bracketing commas set off parenthetical expressions. A parenthetical expression is one that contains information not essential to the main idea of the sentence.

Correct *Keith, who is a lawyer, also reads tarot cards as a hobby.*

The main idea is that Keith reads tarot cards as a hobby. The intervening clause merely serves to identify Keith; thus, it should be set off with commas.

Correct The Tale of Genji, *written in the eleventh century, is considered by literary historians to be the world's first novel.*

The main idea is that *The Tale of Genji* is considered to be the world's first novel. The intervening phrase "written in the eleventh century" merely introduces additional but non-essential information.

Correct *The old brick house that I wanted to buy is now a historical landmark.*

Correct *The old brick house, which the mayor visited last year, is now a historical landmark.*

In the first of the two examples above, "that I wanted to buy" defines which old brick house the author is discussing. In the second example, the main point is that the old brick house is now a historical landmark, and the intervening clause "which the mayor visited last year" merely adds additional but nonessential information.

Commas are also used after introductory participial or prepositional phrases.

> **Correct**   *Having collected rare coins for more than*
> *fifteen years, Bill was heartbroken when his*
> *collection was stolen in a house burglary.*

> **Correct**   *Like those of Sir Isaac Newton, the scientific*
> *contributions of Albert Einstein have proven*
> *monumental.*

JOINING COMMA

Use commas to separate independent clauses connected by coordinating conjunctions such as *and*, *but*, *yet*, *or*, *nor*, *for*. (Independent clauses are clauses that can stand alone as complete sentences.)

> **Correct**   *Susan wants to get her story published, and she*
> *wants to have it made into a movie.*

> **Correct**   *Maurice ate Habanero peppers with every*
> *meal, yet he hardly ever got indigestion.*

OMISSION COMMA

Use commas to indicate missing words, particularly the word *and*.

> **Correct**   *I can't believe you sat through that long, dull,*
> *uninspired lecture without once checking your*
> *watch.*

The above example is correct because the missing word is *and*. We can test this by expressing the sentence as follows: "I can't believe you sat through that long and dull and uninspired lecture without once checking your watch."

> **Incorrect**   *The Tarsier is a small, bug-eyed, timid, crea-*
> *ture that lives in the central Philippines and*
> *parts of Indonesia.*

In the previous example, the comma should not be placed after *timid* because *and* cannot be substituted for it. For instance, the phrase "timid and creature" makes no sense.

> **Incorrect** *It was a juicy ripe mango.*
>
> **Correct** *It was a juicy, ripe mango.*

A comma is required to separate *juicy* from *ripe*. There are two ways to test for this. The first is to substitute *and* for the comma and see if things still make sense. The second is to reverse the word order and see if things still make sense. For example, since we can equally say "ripe, juicy mango," a comma is indeed required.

Exercises

Correct the comma usage in each sentence by observing its four uses: listing, bracketing, joining, or omission. The answers are on pages 158-159.

1. The Oscar the Emmy and the Tony are three related awards which confuse many people.
2. Emerging from the ruins of World War II Japan embarked on an economic recovery that can be only viewed in historical terms as astonishing.
3. Every major band requires, a lead singer, a lead guitarist, a bass guitarist, and a drummer.
4. A dedicated empathetic individual can achieve lifetime recognition as a United Nations worker.
5. I was shocked to discover that a torn, previously worn, garish, piece of Madonna's underwear sold for more money at the auction than did a large, splendid, seventeenth-century sketch by Vignon.

6. The crowded housing tenement, a cluster of rundown, look-alike apartments was the site of the Prime Minister's birthplace.

7. Despite having top analysts capable of weighing objectively the pros and cons of any military option presidents and prime ministers alike find it ostensibly impossible to factor out their subjective feelings when faced with the decision to go to war.

8. South Africa is famous for her gold and diamonds, Thailand for her silk and emeralds, and Brazil for her coffee and sugarcane.

9. She reached for the clock, and finding it, hastily silenced the alarm.

10. Josie originally wanted to be a nurse but after finishing university she decided to become a lawyer instead.

SEMICOLONS

Use a semicolon instead of a coordinate conjunction (*and*, *but*, *yet*, *or*, *nor*, *for*) to link two closely related sentences.

Correct *Students are more creative today, but they are also weaker in the basics of reading, writing, and arithmetic.*

Correct *Students are more creative today; they are also weaker in the basics of reading, writing, and arithmetic.*

Use a semicolon between independent clauses connected by words such as *however*, *therefore*, *moreover*, *nevertheless*, *consequently*. These special words are called conjunctive adverbs.

Incorrect *The formulas for many scientific discoveries appear rudimentary, however, when one examines a derivation behind these formulas they do not seem so rudimentary after all.*

Correct *The formulas for many scientific discoveries appear rudimentary; however, when one examines a derivation behind these formulas they do not seem so rudimentary after all.*

To see commas and semicolons in action, let us introduce a very common error: the run-on sentence. A run-on is two sentences inappropriately joined together, usually by a comma. There are four ways to correct a run-on sentence.

Incorrect *Technology has made our lives easier, it has also made our lives more complicated.*

Method 1: Change the comma to a semicolon.

Correct *Technology has made our lives easier; it has also made our lives more complicated.*

Method 2: Join two sentences with a conjunction.

Correct *Technology has made our lives easier, and it has also made our lives more complicated.*

Method 3: Make two separate sentences.

Correct *Technology has made our lives easier. It has also made our lives more complicated.*

Method 4: Make one of the sentences a subordinate clause.

Correct *Even though technology has made our lives easier, it has also made our lives more complicated.*

Appendix 1. Overview of Principles and Rules

STRUCTURE

Principle 1   Write your conclusion and place it first.

Principle 2   Break your subject into two to four major
                   parts and use a lead sentence.

Principle 3   Use transition words to signal the flow of
                   your writing.

Principle 4   Use the six basic writing structures to put
                   ideas in their proper order.

Principle 5   Finish discussing one topic before going on
                   to discuss other topics.

STYLE

Principle 6   Use specific and concrete words to
                   support what you say.

Principle 7   Add personal examples to make your
                   writing more memorable.

Principle 8   Use simple words to express your ideas.

Principle 9   Make your writing clearer by dividing up
                   long sentences.

Principle 10   Cut out redundancies, excessive
                   qualification, and needless self-reference.

Principle 11   Favor active sentences, not passive
                   sentences.

Principle 12   Avoid nominalizing your verbs and
                   adjectives.

Principle 13	Express a series of items in consistent, parallel form.
Principle 14	Vary the length and beginnings of your sentences.
Principle 15	Write with a positive, personal tone.

READABILITY

Principle 16	Add more space around your writing to increase readability.
Principle 17	Make keywords and phrases stand out.
Principle 18	Use headings and headlines to divide or summarize your writing.
Principle 19	Avoid using the masculine generic to refer to both genders.
Principle 20	Wait until your writing stands still before you call it finished.

GRAMMAR

Rule 1	If *he*, *she*, or *they* can be substituted for the pronoun in context, the correct form is *who*. If *him*, *her*, or *them* can be substituted, the correct form is *whom*.
Rule 2	Indefinite pronouns such as *everybody*, *everyone*, *anyone*, and *anything* are always singular.
Rule 3	Pronouns take their objective form when they are the direct objects of prepositions.
Rule 4	Pronouns take their subjective form when used in direct comparisons.

Rule 5	Do not use a reflexive pronoun if an ordinary personal pronoun will suffice.
Rule 6	The superlative is used when comparing three or more persons or things; the comparative is used when comparing exactly two persons or things.
Rule 7	Singular subjects take singular verbs; plural or compound subjects take plural verbs.
Rule 8	To determine whether a verb that follows an *either ... or* or *neither ... nor* construction is singular or plural, match the verb with the word which immediately follows the word *or* or *nor*.
Rule 9	The subjunctive mood uses the verb *were* instead of *was*.
Rule 10	Use consistent verb tenses.
Rule 11	Gerunds and infinitives are always singular and take singular verbs.
Rule 12	Distinguish between possessives and contractions.
Rule 13	Distinguish between *than* and *then*.
Rule 14	*All together* means in one group. *Altogether* means completely or entirely.
Rule 15	*All ready* means entirely ready or prepared. *Already* means before or previously but may also mean now or so soon.
Rule 16	*Maybe* is an adverb meaning perhaps. *May be* is a verb phrase.

Rule 17	Use *between* to discuss two things. Use *among* to discuss three or more things.
Rule 18	Use *each other* when referring to two people. Use *one another* when referring to more than two people.
Rule 19	*Fewer* refers to things that can be counted, such as people or things. *Less* refers to things that cannot be counted, such as water or sand.
Rule 20	Use *number* when speaking of things that can be counted. Use *amount* when speaking of things that cannot be counted.
Rule 21	*Affect* is a verb meaning to influence; *effect* is a noun meaning result; *effect* is also a verb meaning to bring about.
Rule 22	*That* is used for restrictive clauses; *which* is used for non-restrictive clauses.
Rule 23	Use *farther* when referring to distance. Use *further* in all other situations, particularly when referring to extent or degree.
Rule 24	Use *if* to express one possibility. Use *whether* to express two or more possibilities.
Rule 25	Use *compare to* in pointing out similarities. Use *compare with* in pointing out differences.
Rule 26	Use *differ from* in discussing characteristics. Use *differ with* to convey the idea of disagreement.
Rule 27	*Infer* means to draw a conclusion; readers or

listeners infer. *Imply* means to hint or to suggest; speakers or writers imply.

Rule 28	*Passed* functions as a verb; *past* functions as a noun, adjective, or preposition.
Rule 29	One way to distinguish between *like* and *as* is that *like* is used in phrases whereas *as* is used in clauses.
Rule 30	In the present tense, *lie* means to rest or to recline and *lay* means to put or to place.

Appendix 2. American vs. British English

American English and British English differ according to spelling and punctuation but not grammar. The following chart summarizes the major differences in spelling between American and British English.

American		British	
-a	gage	-au	gauge
-ck	check	-que	cheque
-ed	learned	-t	learnt
-er	center, meter	-re	centre, metre
no *e*	judgment	-e	judgement
no *st*	among	-st	amongst
-in	inquiry	-en	enquiry
-k	disk	-c	disc
-l	traveled	-ll	travelled
-ll	fulfill	-l	fulfil
-m	program	-mme	programme
-o	mold	-ou	mould
-og	catalog	-ogue	catalogue
-or	color	-our	colour
-z	summarize	-s	summarise

Appendix 3. Latin Abbreviations

Latin abbreviations should be used with caution. Their use depends on whether the intended audience is likely to be familiar with their meaning. This compilation is not so much an endorsement for their possible use as it is a convenient list in case readers find them in various works.

Abbreviation	Meaning
c.	approximately
cf.	compare
e.g.	for example
etc.	and so forth
et. al.	and other people
ibid.	in the same place
i.e.	in other words; that is
op. cit.	in the work cited
sc.	which means
sic.	in these exact words
v.	consult
viz.	namely

Appendix 4. Exercise Answers

PRINCIPLE 3 (PAGE 20)

The following is a possible way to organize the whale essay. The sentences are arranged 5, 2, 1, 4, 3.

THE WHALE

The whale is the largest mammal in the animal kingdom. When most people think of whales, they think of sluggish, obese animals, frolicking freely in the ocean and eating tons of food to sustain themselves. When people think of ants, on the other hand, they tend to think of hardworking underfed creatures transporting objects twice their body size to and from hidden hideaways. However, if we analyze food consumption based on body size, we find that ants eat their full body weight everyday, while a whale eats the equivalent of only 1/1,000th of its body weight each day. In fact, when we compare the proportionate food consumption of all living creatures, we find that the whale is one the most food efficient creatures on earth.

> *NOTE* ☞ The conclusion appears in the last line. If a piece is very short and uncomplicated, there is little harm in putting the conclusion at the end. This may seem like an exception to Principle 1, and it is, but it represents the art of writing as opposed to the science of writing.

PRINCIPLE 6 (PAGE 37)

1. Joannie has a German Shepherd and a Siamese cat.

2. The vacation cost nearly $10,000.

3. Amanda often loses her car keys.

4. Many economists think that the Federal Reserve Bank's failure to lower bank interest rates is the reason for the current economic downturn.

5. Firms should use billboard advertising because it is low cost and can increase sales as much as 10 percent in a given region.

6. Sheila is 5'10" tall and has an attractive baby-shaped face.

7. Rainbows contain a full spectrum of colors, including red, orange, yellow, green, indigo, blue, and violet.

8. The student was unable to complete the midterm research report, which was to include ten pages of findings, and five pages of tables, graphs, and appendixes.

9. Fresh produce, small cans, and large boxes line each row of the grocery store from floor to ceiling.

10. Mr. and Mrs. Jones spend most of their time together, often laughing at each other's jokes.

PRINCIPLE 7 (PAGE 51)

- ☞ A good idea is cool!
- ☞ A good idea stands out.
- ☞ A good idea may get a chilly reception.
- ☞ A good idea can easily disappear.
- ☞ A good idea has a big effect on its surroundings.
- ☞ A good idea takes time to form.
- ☞ If you overlook a good idea, it can sink you.
- ☞ You only see part of a good idea because there is more to it than meets the eye.
- ☞ One-tenth of the benefit of a good idea is clearly visible but nine-tenths of the long-term benefits lie below the surface.

PRINCIPLE 8 (PAGE 54)

1. Recent studies suggest that carrot juice is good for you.

2. We expect to use hundreds of reams of copy paper in the next 12 months.

3. This plan will eliminate inefficient business practices.

4. Our schoolchildren's education should emphasize the three Rs—reading, writing, and arithmetic.

5. Only meteorologists can analyze changing climatic conditions.

6. When the poet wrote the second and third stanzas, he must have felt despair. (Or: The poem's second and third stanzas are full of despair.)

7. That is a fine dog.

8. The hurricane destroyed almost all structures along the coastline.

9. While I am against war, I also realize that some situations require the use of military force.

10. Like Napoleon's army that marched on Russia more than a century before, the German army was also unable to successfully invade Russia because its soldiers were inadequately prepared for winter conditions.

> NOTE ☞ The last three examples require cutting out sentences to achieve simplicity. Certain sentences may repeat information that the reader has otherwise gleaned from sentences immediately before or after.

PRINCIPLE 10, EXERCISE 1 (PAGE 62)

1. Employees should adhere to the company dress code.

2. A construction project that large needs an effective manager.

3. That Metropolitan museum remains a significant tourist attraction.

4. The conclusion is that physical and psychological symptoms are intertwined.

5. The promoter's charisma does not mask his poor technical knowledge.

6. The recent trend of government borrowing may create poorer nations.

7. These events—war, recession, and health concerns—have combined to create a crisis.

8. Few people can find novel solutions to problems.

9. She has chosen to work for UNESCO.

10. Negotiation opens many doors to peaceful settlement.

PRINCIPLE 10, EXERCISE 2 (PAGES 62-63)

1. Peter is an exceptional student.

2. You are the best person to decide what you should do with your life.

3. The gas tank is empty.

4. Joey is a slow reader.

5. There are many reasons for the disparity of wealth among the world's nations.

6. Every leader should use diplomacy before resorting to force.

7. In India, I found the best food I have ever eaten.

8. She is an excellent pianist.

9. The Hermitage Museum in St. Petersburg is filled with unique paintings.

10. Auditors should remain independent of the companies that they audit.

PRINCIPLE 10, EXERCISE 3 (PAGE 63)

1. The speaker is lost in details.

2. We ought to pay teachers as much as other professionals such as doctors, lawyers, and engineers.

3. This argument cannot be generalized to most economically deprived individuals.

4. Alcohol is a fine social lubricant.

5. More people would not use the library even if books could be delivered to a person's home free of charge.

6. Freedom of speech does not mean that someone can scream "fire" in a crowded movie theatre and be held blameless.

7. Most individuals want to get rich, but many fail simply because they do not set and follow goals.

8. I am not saying that the opposing argument is without merit. (Or: The argument has merit.)

PRINCIPLE 11 (PAGE 67)

1. In premodern times, inexperienced and ill-equipped practitioners often performed medical surgery.

2. The author makes the main point in the last paragraph.

3. Those who attend motivational courses often need them least, while those who choose not to attend usually need them most.

4. We must relocate the tennis courts so apartment residents can use them.

5. Negotiators ironed out the details of the peace agreement minutes before the deadline.

6. Citizens should generously praise Red Cross volunteers for their efforts.

7. An author's literary agent always reviews book contracts before an author signs them.

8. The school posted test results with no concern for confidentiality.

9. A number of clinical psychologists and marriage experts compiled the report.

10. Without money, staff, and local government support, doctors cannot treat diseases in less developed countries.

> *NOTE* ☞ In examples five, eight, and ten, the suggested solutions involves supplying a subject (i.e., *negotiators*, *school*, and *doctors*).

PRINCIPLE 12 (PAGE 70)

1. Amateur cyclists must work to develop their own training programs.

2. A military leader must be able to decide.

3. The expert panel estimates that implementing the new clean air bill will reduce pollution by 30 percent.

4. According to most dietitians, dieters should avoid fat and reduce carbohydrates as the best way to achieve weight loss.

> *NOTE* ☞ Many nominalized sentences are also written in the passive voice. The solution above cures both problems.

5. He read the critic's review to his surprise.

6. Standardized entrance exams help ensure that students can apply to college and graduate school programs on an equal footing.

7. Celebrities should not air their political views on television.

8. During the dot-com boom, investors never seriously questioned whether traditional accounting formulas should be used to value internet companies.

9. Our supervisor decided to terminate those three employees.

10. Difficult course work and lower grades should not discourage students from pursuing new academic ventures.

PRINCIPLE 13, EXERCISE 1 (PAGES 73-74)

1. All business students learn the basics of accounting, marketing, and manufacturing.

2. The fund manager based his theory on stock performance, on bond performance, and on other leading economic indicators.

3. The witness spoke with seriousness and concern.

4. The requirements for a business degree are not as stringent as those for a medical degree.

5. The dancer taught her understudy how to move, dress, work with choreographers, and deal with photographers.

6. The documentary was interesting and informative.

7. The couple invested their money in stocks, in bonds, and in a piece of real estate.

8. The painting may be done either in watercolors or in oils.

9. Olympic volunteers were ready, able, and quite determined to do a great job.

10. My objections regarding pending impeachment are, first, the personal nature of the matter; second, the partisan nature of the matter.

PRINCIPLE 13, EXERCISE 2 (PAGE 76)

1. Cannelloni has been and always will be my favorite Italian dish.

2. Sheila is intrigued with but not very proficient at hand writing analysis.

3. Massage creates a relaxing, therapeutic, and rejuvenating experience both for your body and for your well-being.

4. Brian will not ask for nor listen to any advice.

5. The cross-examination neither contributed to nor detracted from the defendant's claim of innocence.

6. A good scientist not only thinks thoroughly but also thinks creatively.

7. We either forget our plans, or accept their proposal.

8. In addition to having more protein than meat does, the soybean has protein of higher quality than that in meat.

9. A dilemma facing many young professionals is whether to work for money or to work for enjoyment.

10. One should neither lie to another person nor be so blunt as to cause them embarrassment.

PRINCIPLE 14 (PAGE 80)

1. *With a Subject:* <u>Selling</u> is difficult and requires both practical experience and personal initiative.

2. *With a Phrase:* <u>For many reasons</u>, selling is difficult.

3. *With a Clause:* <u>Because it requires both practical experience and personal initiative</u>, selling is difficult.

4. *With a Verb:* <u>Learn</u> to use your experience and your instincts and you will succeed in a selling career.

5. *With an Adverb:* <u>Traditionally</u>, the terms "sales" and "marketing" were used interchangeably.

6. *With Adjectives:* <u>Confident and resourceful</u>, a salesperson must possess these two key traits.

7. *With a Gerund:* <u>Requiring</u> a person to have both practical experience and personal initiative, selling is difficult.

8. *With an Infinitive:* <u>To be</u> an effective salesperson, one must be able to accept disappointment and work in an unpredictable environment.

9. *With Correlative Conjunctions:* <u>Not only</u> practical experience <u>but also</u> personal initiative is required to be a good salesperson.

PRINCIPLE 15 (PAGE 85)

When making the letter more positive, eliminate negative words such as *not able* and *so massive*. Also add personal pronouns such as *you* and *yours*. Moreover, "our company" sounds better than "Comptronics"; "our service department" sounds better than "the service department." The original letter contains two pronouns (*your, they*); the letter on the next page has ten.

Dear Mr. Jones:

Our company deeply regrets hearing of your problems experienced with your notebook computer, Model 1580J. Our engineers have examined the unit and believe that the best solution involves one of two choices:

(1) you receive a full refund on the unit, or

(2) you allow us to replace your computer with a new model.

Please let our service department know your decision.

GRAMMAR EXERCISES (PAGES 116-118)

1a. The woman <u>who</u> is responsible for city planning is Mrs. Green.

> *NOTE* ☞ *She* is responsible for city planning. Since the pronoun *she* can be substituted in context, the correct pronoun is *who*.

1b. This gift is intended for <u>whom</u>?

> *NOTE* ☞ The gift is intended for *him* or *her*. Since the pronouns *him* or *her* can be substituted in context, the correct pronoun is *whom*.

2a. Everybody should mind <u>his or her</u> own business.

> *NOTE* ☞ *Everyone* is an indefinite pronoun which is always singular. Thus, *his* (or *her*) is correct, not *their*.

2b. Few of the students <u>are</u> ready for the test.

> *NOTE* ☞ *Few* is an indefinite pronoun which is always plural. Thus the correct verb is *are*, not *is*.

2c. None of the candidates <u>have</u> any previous political experience.

> *NOTE* ☞ *None* is an indefinite pronoun which can be either singular or plural. Here *candidates* is plural, so the correct verb is *have*, not *has*.

2d. None of the story <u>makes</u> sense.

NOTE ☞ *None* is an indefinite pronoun which can be either singular or plural. Here *story* is singular, so the correct verb is *have*, not *has*.

3a. Between you and <u>me</u>, this plan makes a lot of sense.

NOTE ☞ Pronouns take the objective form when they are the direct object of prepositions. The preposition here is *between*.

3b. People like you and <u>me</u> should know better.

NOTE ☞ The objective form of the pronoun me must follow the preposition *like*.

3c. Will you come and speak to Cecelia and <u>me</u>?

NOTE ☞ The objective form of the pronoun *me* must follow the preposition *to*.

3d. Do not ask for <u>whom</u> the bell tolls.

NOTE ☞ Pronouns take the objective form when they are the direct object of prepositions. The preposition here is *for*.

3e. Come celebrate the New Year with Christina and <u>me</u>.

NOTE ☞ The objective form of the pronoun *me* must follow the preposition *with*.

4a. He is taller than <u>I</u>.

NOTE ☞ In order to test this: "He is taller than *I am*," not "He is taller than *me am*."

4b. My sister sings better than <u>she</u>.

NOTE ☞ In order to test this: "My sister sings better than *she does*," not "My sister sings better than *her does*."

5a. Young Robert hurt <u>himself</u> while climbing alone.

NOTE ☞ We can't say Robert *hurt him* while climbing alone.

5b. The teacher told Julie and <u>me</u> to stop copying.

> *NOTE* ☞ The reflexive pronoun *myself* is not necessary given that the simple pronoun *me* works in context.

6a. Between Tom and Brenda, Tom is the <u>better</u> student.

> *NOTE* ☞ *Better*, the comparative form, is used for two students.

6b. Among all the students, Jeff is the <u>best</u> in math.

> *NOTE* ☞ The superlative *best* is used for three or more students.

7a. The president and key members of his cabinet <u>were</u> present at the meeting.

> *NOTE* ☞ The word *and* creates a compound subject and the verb *were* (not *was*) is required.

7b. The purpose of the executive, administrative, and legislative branches of government <u>is</u> to provide a system of checks and balances.

> *NOTE* ☞ The subject of the sentence is *purpose*. The prepositional phrase "of the executive, administrative, and legislative branches of government" in no way affects verb choice.

8a. Either Yohan or Cecilia <u>is</u> qualified to act as manager.

> *NOTE* ☞ *Cecilia* is singular, so the singular verb is required.

8b. Neither Julie nor her sisters <u>are</u> going on vacation.

> *NOTE* ☞ *Her sisters* are plural, so the plural verb are is required.

9a. If I <u>were</u> you, I would be feeling optimistic.

> *NOTE* ☞ The verb *were* (not *was*) is used to indicate a hypothetical, contrary-to-fact situation.

9b. Sometimes she wishes she <u>were</u> on a tropical island, enjoying drinks at sunset.

NOTE ☞ The subjunctive is used to express a wish; the verb *were* (not *was*) is required.

10a. My dog <u>barks</u> as soon as he sees our neighbor's cat.

> *NOTE* ☞ Simple present tense.

10b. Yesterday afternoon, without warning, smoked <u>filled</u> the sky and sirens sounded.

> *NOTE* ☞ Simple past tense. Both events occurred in the past—*filled* and *sounded*.

10c. Tomorrow, I will <u>go</u> to the party.

> *NOTE* ☞ Simple future tense.

10d. Larry, who <u>had studied</u> Russian for five years, went to work in Moscow.

> *NOTE* ☞ Past perfect tense. A sequence of past tense events is indicated and the past perfect tense is triggered, requiring the use of *had*. Larry first studied then he went to Moscow.

10e. A recent study has found that many workers <u>have</u> opted for lower pay in exchange for more days off.

> *NOTE* ☞ Present perfect tense—a recent study *has found* and workers *have opted*.

10f. By the time I call her, she <u>will have</u> left the office.

> *NOTE* ☞ Future perfect tense. A sequence of future events is indicated and the future perfect tense is triggered. The call is a future event which will occur before another future event—her leaving the office.

11a. Implementing the consultants' recommendations <u>is</u> difficult.

> *NOTE* ☞ "Implementing the consultants' recommendations" is a gerund phrase. Gerund phrases are always singular.

11b. Entertaining multiple goals <u>makes</u> a person's life stressful.

> *NOTE* ❧ "Entertaining multiple goals" is a gerund phrase; the singular verb *makes* is required, not the plural verb *make*.

PUNCTUATION EXERCISES (PAGES 135-136)

1. The Oscar, the Emmy, and the Tony are three related awards which confuse many people.

> *NOTE* ❧ The comma after *Emmy* is optional; in practice it is used in American English but omitted in British English.

2. Emerging from the ruins of World War II, Japan embarked on an economic recovery that can be only viewed in historical terms as astonishing.

> *NOTE* ❧ A bracketing comma is required after *World War II*.

3. Every major band requires a lead singer, a lead guitarist, a bass guitarist, and a drummer.

> *NOTE* ❧ There is no comma after *requires*; the comma after *bass guitarist* is optional.

4. A dedicated, empathetic individual can achieve lifetime recognition as a United Nations worker.

> *NOTE* ❧ An omission comma separates *dedicated* and *empathetic*. There are two ways to test for this. First, substitute the word *and* to read *dedicated and empathetic*. Second, reverse the order of the two words to read *empathetic and dedicated*. Since substituting the word *and* or reversing the word order still makes sense, a comma should be used.

5. I was shocked to discover that a torn, previously worn, garish piece of Madonna's underwear sold for more money at the auction than did a large, splendid, seventeenth-century sketch by Vignon.

> *NOTE* ❧ There are no commas after *garish* or *century*.

6. That crowded housing tenement, a cluster of rundown, look-alike apartments, was the site of the Prime Minister's birthplace.

> *NOTE* ❧ Insert a comma after *apartments*; the parenthetical phrase "a cluster of rundown, look-alike apartments" is nonessential.

7. Despite having top analysts capable of weighing objectively the pros and cons of any military option, presidents and prime ministers alike find it ostensibly impossible to factor out their subjective feelings when faced with the decision to go to war.

> *NOTE* ❧ A bracketing comma after *option* is required.

8. South Africa is famous for her gold and diamonds, Thailand, for her silk and emeralds, and Brazil, for her coffee and sugarcane.

> *NOTE* ❧ A comma is needed after *Thailand* and *Brazil*. Such a comma takes the place of *is famous*. So, the sentence might read: "South Africa is famous for her gold and diamonds, Thailand is famous for her silk and emeralds, and Brazil is famous for her coffee and sugarcane."

9. She reached for the clock and, finding it, hastily silenced the alarm.

> *NOTE* ❧ A bracketing comma is needed before and after the words *finding it*; this is a nonessential phrase. To see this error more clearly, re-read the original sentence after first removing the words contained within commas: "She reached for the clock hastily silenced the alarm."

10. Josie originally wanted to be a nurse, but after finishing university, she decided to become a lawyer instead.

> *NOTE* ❧ A joining comma is required before *but* while a bracketing comma is required after *university*. Note that, per the solution, the two commas above do not both function as bracketing commas; if this were so we could cut out the phrase "but after finishing university" and the sentence would still make sense, but it doesn't: "Josie originally wanted to be a nurse she decided to become a lawyer instead."

ABOUT THE AUTHOR

As an author, speaker, and education consultant, Brandon draws upon an eclectic background having worked across a wide-range of industries including oil and gas, high tech, public accounting, education, teaching, corporate training, and publishing.

As a former joint-venture auditor for the Ernst and Young accounting group, he audited client companies including Coca-Cola, McCormick Seasoning and Foodstuffs Company, and the Hilton and Holiday Inn Hotels in China. As a corporate trainer, he has conducted seminars for such well-known organizations as AT&T, ATKearney, Merrill Lynch, and JPMorgan. During his tenure with US-based Kaplan Educational Centers—a Washington Post subsidiary and the oldest and largest test preparatory organization in the world—Brandon honed his teaching skills and developed an expertise in graduate business school admissions strategies.

A Canadian by birth and a resident of Hong Kong, Brandon's interest in writing began after completing fiction and scriptwriting courses at Harvard University. Since then he has authored seven books and written across a diverse spectrum, penning fiction, non-fiction, short stories, essays, news articles, speeches, poetry, and personal quotations. In his own words, he is light-hearted but not long-winded: "I am an accountant by training, an anthropologist by disposition, a writer by choice, and a bar patron by preference."

Other books by Brandon Royal include: *The Little Green Math Book, The Little Blue Reasoning Book, Ace the GMAT, A Perfect MBA Application, Bars of Steel,* and *Pleasure Island.*

To contact the author:
E-mail: brandon@brandonroyal.com
Web site: www.brandonroyal.com